American Revolutionary War

Continental
VERSUS
Redcoat

COMBAT

David Bonk

First published in Great Britain in 2014 by Osprey Publishing,
PO Box 883, Oxford, OX1 9PL, UK
PO Box 3985, New York, NY 10185-3985, USA
E-mail: info@ospreypublishing.com

Osprey Publishing is part of the Osprey Group

© 2014 Osprey Publishing Ltd.

A CIP catalog record for this book is available from the British Library

Print ISBN: 978 1 4728 0648 2
PDF ebook ISBN: 978 1 4728 0649 9
ePub ebook ISBN: 978 14728 0650 5

Index by Zoe Ross
Typeset in Univers, Sabon and Adobe Garamond Pro
Maps by bounford.com
Originated by PDQ Media, Bungay, UK
Printed in China through Asia Pacific Offset Ltd

15 16 17 18   10 9 8 7 6 5 4 3 2

Osprey Publishing is supporting the Woodland Trust, the UK's leading
woodland conservation charity, by funding the dedication of trees.

www.ospreypublishing.com

Dedication

To my wife Jackie, to whom I am eternally grateful for her support and
encouragement.

Acknowledgments

Thanks to Michael Timpanaro at the Monmouth battlefield and Andrew
Outten at the Brandywine battlefield for their help, and John Robertson
and Dr. Bob McCaskill for the tour of the Cowpens battlefield. Thanks
are also due to the Anne S.K. Brown Military Collection, Brown
University Library (ASKB) and the Military & Historical Image Bank,
who generously provided so many of the illustrations.

Editor's note

US customary (UK imperial) units of measurement are used in this
study. For ease of comparison please refer to the following conversion
table:

1 mile = 1.6km
1yd = 0.9m
1ft = 0.3m
1in = 2.54cm/25.4mm
1lb = 0.45kg

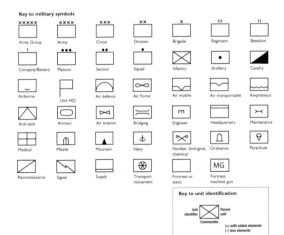

CONTENTS

Introduction

The history of the American Revolutionary War (1775–83) has been steeped in nationalistic myth and much we know about the conflict tends to focus on the larger-than-life personalities such as General George Washington, Lieutenant-General Sir Henry Clinton, or General Sir William Howe. Beyond that handful of recognizable names we know little about the lives and struggles of senior officers such as Nathanael Greene, Anthony Wayne, or Sir Charles Grey. We know even less about the men who fought in the ranks to secure their independence, or who fought for their King. Much of the written record of the war has been left by officers in the form of diaries and post-war memoirs. There were rare enlisted soldiers on both sides who kept diaries or corresponded regularly with family. It is interesting to note that for both officers and lower ranks their writing tended to focus on mundane daily activities – food, accommodation, how far and where they marched – rather than descriptions of combat. When they did write about combat it was surprisingly cursory. Using those available resources we have sought to describe the experience of three battles through the recollections of individual soldiers.

The American Revolutionary War was fought across a broad landscape, ranging from the frozen forests of northern New York to the humid backcountry of the Carolinas. The geography and climate of the American colonies largely dictated the strategy and tactics of the Revolutionary War. While British tactical doctrine, as embodied in the 1764 Regulations, did reflect an emphasis on linear tactics based on a three-rank formation, the army that engaged the American patriots around Boston in 1775 was in transition. The evolution of British tactics in North America can be traced back to their experience in the French and Indian War fought against France between 1754 and 1763. That experience led key members of the British military leadership, many of whom had fought in the war, to develop innovative approaches to the deployment and operations of their armies. This included following the

practice used in Europe of organizing light infantry and grenadier companies into composite battalions and the adoption of different formations that involved reducing the number of ranks from three to two and requiring greater separation between the men in the lines. As the war progressed British commanders revised and adapted their tactics, including the formations they used, to better address local conditions and their enemy.

The initial approach of the American military leadership to both tactics and doctrine reflected the unique attributes of the men who volunteered to serve. It was also influenced by the experience many senior commanders had while serving with their British counterparts during the French and Indian War. As the war progressed the American commanders trained their men to fight in the more rigid formations, while British practice stressed more open formations, so that by the end of the war both sides had adopted a wide range of options.

The three examples of combat presented here, providing examples of combat between British regulars and American Continental infantry, have been selected to provide insights into the evolution of tactics and the ingenuity of commanders on both sides in adapting their tactics to the situation on the ground. At Brandywine on September 11, 1777, although surprised by the British flanking movement, the American Continentals were able to respond, thereby delaying the British advance and allowing the army to retire. Brigadier General George Weedon's brigade marched in haste but retained their order despite the confusion caused by the retreat of Major General John Sullivan's

This engraving of the battle of Lexington by Amos Doolittle (1754–1832) shows Major John Pitcairn commanding British grenadiers in the battle. Pitcairn would be mortally wounded at Bunker Hill only weeks later. The popular image of combat during the Revolutionary War is of British redcoats marching in lockstep in massed formations against American militia and riflemen who fought from behind walls and trees. The reality of combat between the British and Americans over the course of the conflict was very different, however. (ASKB)

Infantry: Continental Army, 1779–1783, IV by Henry Alexander Ogden (1856–1936), *c.*1897. In January 1779 Washington submitted a proposal to the Continental Congress for the standardization of uniforms, suggesting each state adopt a different color uniform, with facing colors distinguishing different units. He also suggested pants be replaced with woolen overalls for winter and linen for summer wear. Congress passed along the proposal to the Board of War, which responded in May 1779 with a revised plan adopting dark blue as the standard uniform color and dividing the states into four groups, each with a different facing color. The proposed facing colors were white (New Hampshire, Massachusetts, Rhode Island, and Connecticut), buff (New York and New Jersey), red (Pennsylvania, Delaware, Maryland, and Virginia), and blue with white lace button-holes (North Carolina, South Carolina, and Georgia). (Library of Congress)

command. The steadiness of the 2nd Virginia during the twilight battle matched the discipline shown by the British 64th Regiment in exchanging fire at close range in the growing darkness. Despite the stubborn defense of the Birmingham Meeting House by the 3rd Virginia Regiment the lack of combat experience, particularly among the senior commanders, and the sheer weight of the British advance threatened to overwhelm the American line. At Monmouth Courthouse on June 28, 1778 the Continentals marched to battle with greater confidence in their training while the British again showed their tactical dexterity by deftly moving from defense to offense. After rigorous training at Valley Forge during the winter of 1777–78 the Continentals were better able to respond to the shifting tactical situation and engage their enemies on equal terms. The British exhibited tactical finesse in shifting quickly from the defense to an aggressive attack that threw the Americans into confusion and caused a precipitous retreat, while command errors on both sides overshadowed the bravery of the soldiers. The battle of Cowpens on January 17, 1781, marked a turning point in the British campaign to secure the Southern states. By this time American Continental units such as the Delaware Continentals were composed largely of hardened veterans, well trained and able to stand toe to toe with their British opponents. At the same time the long war, which resulted in continuing attrition to British units, diminished the capabilities of those regiments, such as the 7th Royal Fusiliers, that found themselves with untested replacements. Ultimately, as in all the examples, the quality of command decided the day.

The American Revolutionary War

The American Revolutionary War was fought over a broad expanse of the eastern portion of North America, reaching up into Canada and down to Florida. The focus of combat operations shifted during the course of the conflict, beginning in New England and then extending west into New York and south into New Jersey. After an initial unsuccessful British attempt to capture Charleston, the third-largest city in the newly formed United States, both sides conducted major military operations in the area between Philadelphia and New York during between 1776 and 1778. The American defeat at Brandywine in September 1777 led to the British capture of Philadelphia. In June 1778 the British abandoned Philadelphia and during the retreat back to New York were attacked by American forces at Monmouth Courthouse. Beginning in 1779 the focus of British strategy was to move the war into the Southern states where it was thought Loyalists would flock to the King's colors. Despite the capture of Charleston in 1780 the British were unsuccessful in securing the backcountry, suffering a defeat at Cowpens in January 1781. With the British unable to destroy American continental forces and secure the Carolinas or Virginia, in October 1781 a joint American–French army forced British Lieutenant-General Charles Earl Cornwallis to surrender at Yorktown, Virginia, ending major combat operations in America.

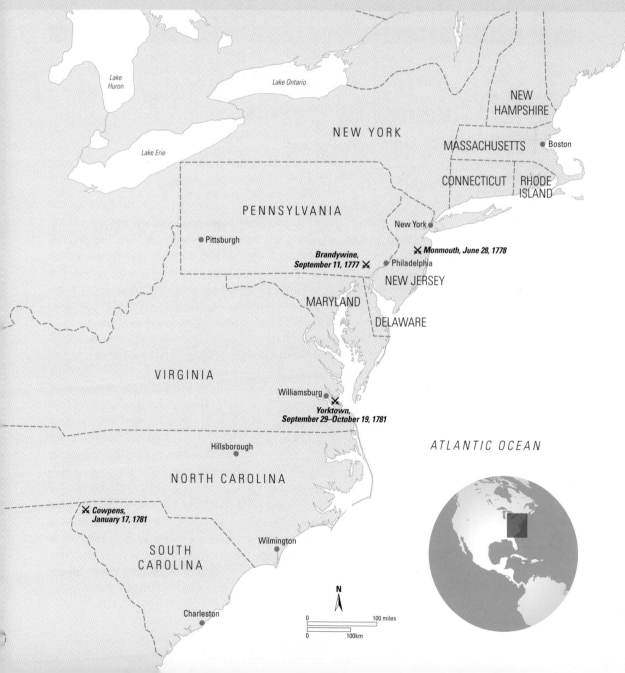

The Opposing Sides

RECRUITMENT AND ORGANIZATION

British

British recruits were largely motivated by economic necessity. The financial bounty for enlistment started out at a guinea (£1 1d) but was increased to £3 in 1778. In addition the recruit received the "King's Shilling," which was actually a crown. Out of the bounty the recruit was required to pay for kit and clothing. Similarly, the monthly pay of soldiers was offset by deductions for food, shoes, stockings, repair of muskets, and a host of other spurious expenses, leaving the soldier with virtually nothing. As voluntary recruitment became more difficult, in 1778 and 1779 the British government invoked the Press Act, which allowed them to forcibly draft men into the Army. Most affected by this were the poorest, those who were subsisting "on the parish" for charity.

At the beginning of the war the basic battlefield infantry unit for both the British and Americans was the regiment, which was normally composed of one battalion. (During this period the use of the designations regiment and battalion was largely interchangeable.) The British organized most regular infantry regiments as a single battalion of ten companies: eight center companies, a company of light infantry, and a grenadier company. Generally, men assigned to the grenadier and light-infantry companies were chosen based on their physical stamina and physique. The grenadiers, intended to be utilized as shock troops, were selected for their large size, while the candidates for the light infantry were usually smaller in stature. Both the grenadier and light-infantry companies were usually grouped together with those from other regiments into composite battalions. Some regiments raised more than one battalion. For example, the 42nd (Royal Highland) Regiment, which fought at Brandywine and Monmouth Courthouse, raised a second battalion in

1780. The cumbersomely named 71st Regiment of (Highland) Foot (Fraser's) raised two battalions in 1775, both of which fought in North America, and added a third in 1777; all three fought at Brandywine and elements of the regiment were present at Cowpens.

Although some units fielded all three troop types – Brigadier-General Edward Mathew's Guards Brigade, which fought at Brandywine and Monmouth Courthouse, grouped ten companies, including a light company and a grenadier company, in two composite battalions – it was customary to detach the light and grenadier companies and form them into composite battalions that operated independently. At Brandywine, the light companies of 28 different regiments were formed into two light-infantry battalions, while no fewer than 31 grenadier companies were assigned to the two grenadier battalions that saw action at Brandywine and Monmouth Courthouse. Light companies could also operate as individual units; for example, the Light Company of the Guards Brigade fought independently. Light companies could also operate as individual units when deployed with their parent regiments in smaller detachments where the entire force was composed of only a few regiments. Each company had a paper strength of a captain, two lieutenants, two sergeants, three corporals, 38 privates, a drummer and a fifer. Total battalion strength, with flank companies, was 480 plus command personnel. Command staff consisted of a colonel, lieutenant-colonel, adjutant – typically a major or captain – chaplain, and a surgeon and surgeon's mate.

During the course of the war the British also formed more than 150 Loyalist units throughout America and Canada. Provincial units were the equivalent of American Continental units and were given the same pay, uniforms, and provisions as regular British units. British officers and sergeants were assigned to the Provincial units to bolster their training and leadership. Five Provincial regiments were awarded the special status of being placed on the "American Establishment." This designation was given to units that met

ABOVE
British infantry officers, 1775. Depending on rank and unit, British officers wore either one (right) or two epaulettes; these were either gold or silver, according to the color of the regimental metal. Officers also wore a metal gorget, gold or silver, around the neck and a crimson silk sash around the waist. Sergeants also wore a sash, but with a center stripe of the regimental facing color. At left is an officer of grenadiers armed with a fusil, a shortened version of the Short Land Service musket with a 42in barrel, while at right is a center-company officer with spontoon, a polearm with a spear head mounted on a long shaft. In 1770 officers of fusilier regiments were authorized to carry an officer's fusil. In 1776 the use of the officer's fusil was allowed for Highland and Guards officers and by the end of the war it had been adopted unofficially by most officers. Although the grenadier companies carried their bearskins through the early years of the war they were eventually replaced by cocked or round hats as a matter of convenience. (ASKB)

An American recruiting broadside. Joseph Plumb Martin described how patriotic enthusiasm and monetary reward combined in 1775: "A dollar was deposited upon the drumhead and was taken up by someone as soon as it was placed there, and the holders name taken, and he enrolled with orders to equip himself as quick as possible." Martin, who was considering enlisting at the time, noted that, "My spirits began to revive at the sight of the money offered; the seeds of courage began to sprout ... O, thought I, if I were but old enough to put myself forward, I would be in possession of one dollar, the dangers of war to the contrary notwithstanding ..." (quoted in Martin 1993: 7). Martin did finally enlist in July 1776 for a term expiring on December 25, 1776. (Library of Congress)

their recruitment goals or acquitted themselves well on the battlefield. A total of seven Provincial units, including the five from the American Establishment, were placed on the Regular Establishment. These included the Royal Highland Emigrants, Queen's Rangers, Volunteers of Ireland, New York Volunteers, King's American Regiment, British Legion, and the Newfoundland Regiment. Other Loyalist units, similar in nature to American State troops, were recruited by individual British governors. These units were not considered part of the Army and were not extended the same benefits provided to Provincial units. British governors also established militia units, drawn from able-bodied males between the ages of 16 and 60. Volunteer militia units were often provided with uniforms and pay similar to those of British troops, while conscripted militia units were required to provide their own arms and provisions.

American

Like his British counterpart the typical American recruit responded to economic incentives. In 1776 men were offered a $10 signing bonus and monthly pay of $62/3 (40 shillings). By the spring of 1777 the bounty had doubled to $20 and 100 acres of land promised at the end of the war. Despite the incentives it continued to be a challenge to recruit enough soldiers. Washington urged a draft of militia for a 12-month enlistment. By 1778 every state had some form of draft. The draft was a lottery, with each militia

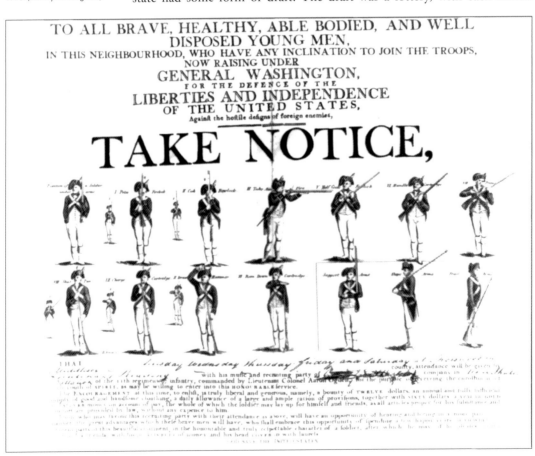

TO ALL BRAVE, HEALTHY, ABLE BODIED, AND WELL DISPOSED YOUNG MEN,
IN THIS NEIGHBOURHOOD, WHO HAVE ANY INCLINATION TO JOIN THE TROOPS,
NOW RAISING UNDER
GENERAL WASHINGTON,
FOR THE DEFENCE OF THE
LIBERTIES AND INDEPENDENCE
OF THE UNITED STATES,
Against the hostile designs of foreign enemies,

TAKE NOTICE,

Published in 1770, this engraving by Paul Revere (1735–1818) shows the bloody clash between the 29th Regiment of Foot and the local population in Boston on March 5, 1770. Although the financial incentives proved the strongest motivation for Continental recruits, some enlisted out of sense of idealism or political interest in protecting their rights as they defined them. In some cases a sense of adventure led to enlistment. Washington understood that the revolutionary spirit that attracted men early in the conflict would not last: "I do not exclude altogether the Idea of Patriotism. I know it exists … But I venture to assert, that a great and lasting War can never be supported on this principle alone. It must be aided by a prospect of Interest or some reward. For a time, it may, of itself push Men to Action; to bear much, to encounter difficulties; but it will not endure unassisted by Interest" (quoted in Higginbotham 1985: 89). (ASKB)

regiment given a quota that helped fulfill the state's obligation to the regular army. Men were selected by the militia colonel, usually by random selection. Upon selection the soldier could pay a fine and be relieved of the obligation, or pay a substitute. Forced conscription was used on indentured servants, vagrants, and criminals.

During the war there were three classes of American troops: Continentals, State troops, and militia. The Continental Congress authorized the formation of the Continental units in June 1775. The Congress adopted regulations for the pay, supply, and terms of service for Continental units throughout the war as well as raising additional formations. State units were raised by individual state legislatures or governors by voluntary enlistment for a specific period of time, usually in response to a specific threat. While the terms of enlistment stipulated these troops would only operate within the boundaries of the individual state, in some instances they could be deployed in adjacent states for a specified period of time. As the war progressed many State units, as well as militia formations, included a significant number of former Continental veterans whose terms of enlistment had expired or who had been mustered out of service. Militia units usually represented a standing force mustered around a specific geographic area such as a county or township. Although there were exemptions, typically all able-bodied men aged between 16 and 65 were expected to serve.

While the hastily organized militia enjoyed some success early in the war and would continue to play an important role in individual campaigns it was the Continental units that formed the backbone of the American Army. It was around this core that state and militia units could muster as needed. General George Washington was an early proponent of creating a standing army made up of Continental units, despite the concerns raised by political leaders. Washington wrote in 1776 to John Hancock, President of the Continental Congress:

> To place any dependence upon militia, is, assuredly, resting upon a broken staff. Men just dragged from the tender scenes of domestic life unaccustomed to the din of arms; totally unacquainted with every kind of military skill, which followed by a

want of confidence in themselves, when opposed in Troops regularly trained, disciplined, and appointed superior in knowledge, and superior in arms, makes them timid and ready to fly from their own shadow. (Quoted in McCullough 2001: 159)

The Americans also adopted the regiment, composed of one battalion, as their basic infantry formation. Regulations adopted in late September 1776 stipulated that each American battalion was to be led by a colonel, assisted by a lieutenant colonel and major. The command staff was composed of ten men, including a quartermaster, surgeon, chaplain, and sergeant major. The battalion was to be comprised of eight companies; each company was led by a captain and included two lieutenants, an ensign, four sergeants, four corporals, a drummer, a fifer, and 76 privates for a total strength of 90 men. The paper strength of each battalion was 733 men, although throughout the course of the war most units operated with far fewer personnel.

Unlike the British the Americans did not include light companies or grenadier companies in the regimental organization; at the beginning of the conflict some local units were organized and outfitted as grenadiers but these formations largely disappeared by early 1776. In the first few years of the war units of American riflemen undertook the same role as British light infantry, conducting general reconnaissance and acting as the advance guard during the march. During the war General George Washington raised light-infantry formations composed of "picked men," usually veterans, which operated in several different roles. During the 1777 Saratoga campaign American forces included both a rifle corps and a light-infantry formation, both of which were deployed in a light-infantry role. For the 1779 raid against the British at Stony Point, Major General Anthony Wayne commanded a light-infantry corps that was utilized more as shock troops than light infantry. During 1781, Major General Marquis de Lafayette commanded a light-infantry corps that operated in Virginia as an independent unit. Throughout the course of the war American commanders organized ad hoc units of "select men," usually veterans drawn from different regiments or brigades, to act as light infantry. Some units also took on the title of light infantry to reflect their veteran status and ability to operate in different formations. It was not until late in the war that officially designated units of light infantry were organized. American riflemen and militia units operated as light infantry in part due to their weaponry or lack of formal training.

UNIFORMS, EQUIPMENT, AND WEAPONS

British

Like their tactics the uniforms of the British soldiers fighting in America went through an evolution throughout the course of the war. The standard British infantryman began the war wearing a red coat made of wool. The coat had cuffs, lapels, and collars in the regimental color. The tails of the coat were secured up, exposing the white lining. The soldier wore a vest, usually of white, and white pants secured just below the knee. White stockings and black shoes and a black tricorne hat completed the uniform. Throughout the course of the war British soldiers adapted their uniforms in response to battlefield conditions, climate, and ultimately the limited availability of resupply. Major-General John Burgoyne's army operating in the rugged forests of Lower Canada and upstate New York cut down their coats to ease their movement through the dense forests. Overalls, which were more practical, replaced the shorter pants for all troops as the war progressed.

The official British marching order included knapsack and blanket, haversack for rations, water canteen, musket, bayonet, and ammunition, together weighing over 60lb. In addition tin camp kettles, one assigned for each group of five men, were carried. The rigors of campaigning in the field soon gave way to utilitarian decisions to trade backpacks for blanket rolls and use haversacks to carry several days' precooked provisions. Ammunition was administered by the Royal Artillery while each battalion maintained a supply of 100 rounds per man. Each soldier carried 60 rounds in a cartridge box and haversack, while the remainder was assigned to the regimental baggage. The British provided a daily ration of up to 1lb of meat and 1lb of bread, supplemented by butter, rice, and cheese and other "small species." In the field the ration could be increased to 1½lb of bread and 1½lb meat, although the bread was usually prebaked hard biscuits. Also provided was a daily gill of rum.

American

American uniforms were generally more varied than those of their opponents, owing in part to a lack of resources and in part to the manner the troops were raised and organized. With the start of the war in 1775 units were clothed in a wide variety of styles and colors, although the bulk of the men were dressed in their civilian clothes. General George Washington believed that hunting shirts should serve as the official uniform and encouraged the American Congress to provide the necessary supplies. While Congress agreed that the hunting shirt provided an alternative they continued to insist on more orthodox dress. The arrival of large shipments of uniforms from France in 1778 helped alleviate the shortages, although the coats were both blue and brown, faced in red. Throughout the war the hunting shirt continued to be distributed either due to shortages or for more practical reasons.

Early in the war Americans were armed with a wide variety of older or captured British weapons. Troops from the Pennsylvania, Maryland, and Virginia backcountry brought rifles, which were virtually unknown to the New England men. Washington quickly realized standardization of weapons was needed, but little resources the men continued to use whatever weapon they brought. In other cases recruits showed up with no weapons and the Americans were hard pressed to fill the gap. When enlistments expired the men left with their weapons and in many cases with the muskets they had been given. In November 1775 the Continental Congress issued specifications for the manufacture of muskets, referred to as the Committee of Safety model, based on the British Brown Bess musket:

ABOVE

A British sergeant's iron-hilted hanger. British officers of major and above were authorized to carry swords of their own choosing, while officers below the rank of major (and sergeants) were issued a short sword. During the French and Indian War British sergeants had exchanged their halberds for muskets. The halberd, which consisted of a decorative axe blade topped with a spike, mounted on a long shaft, was both representative of rank and used by the sergeants to realign the ranks of men. In 1770 sergeants in the grenadier companies were issued a special-pattern fusil, which was a scaled-down version of the Short Land Service Pattern musket, with a 39in barrel. Later in 1770 sergeants of light-infantry companies were also issued the same fusil; sergeants in battalion companies continued to use the halberd. (Image courtesy of the Military & Historical Image Bank)

OPPOSITE

During the Revolutionary War British troops were armed with the ubiquitous Brown Bess flintlock musket, which would see use for over a century, over which time 7.8 million were manufactured. The King's or Tower musket, known as the Long Land Service pattern, became general issue in the 1720s. This 1756-pattern Long Land musket is marked to the 23rd Regiment of Foot (Royal Welsh Fuziliers). In 1740 the Short Land Service model modified the gun by shortening the barrel by 4in, to 3ft 6in. (Image courtesy of the Military & Historical Image Bank)

A French M1774 infantry musket surcharged twice "United States," indicating usage by American forces. After 1777 large quantities of French muskets were used to arm the Americans although it seems that there was a preference for the British musket over the French Charleville model. William Lloyd, a New Jersey militiaman, recounted the aftermath of a skirmish near Freehold in 1778: "The enemy then retreating precipitately, throwing away many of their guns. I was, I believe, the foremost in following, got as many of their guns as I could conveniently manage on my horse, with their bayonets fixed upon them. Gave them to the soldiers as they stood in rank. They threw away their French pieces, preferring the British" (quoted in Dann 1980: 124–25). (Image courtesy of the Military & Historical Image Bank)

Resolved. That it be recommended to the several Assemblies or conventions of the colonies respectively, to set up and keep their gunsmiths at work, to manufacture good fire locks, with bayonets; each fire lock to be made with a good bridle lock, ¾ of an inch bore, and of good substance at the breech, the barrel to be 3 feet 8 inches in length, the bayonet to be 18 inches in the blade, with steel ramrod, the upper loop thereof to be a trumpet mounted; the price to be given be fixed by the Assembly or convention, or committee of safety of each colony. (Quoted in Peterson 1956: 183)

After 1777 the primary source of American arms became the importation of the French Charleville musket, with over 23,000 delivered through the course of the war. The French musket was sturdy, although it fired a ball of small caliber (.69in), had less punch than the Brown Bess, and fouled more quickly, requiring more frequent cleaning.

DRILL MANUALS AND TACTICS

British

The basic infantry formation, prescribed in the British Army 1764 Regulations, was the line, in which the battalion should draw up in three ranks. The company was the basic administrative subunit and in the field most maneuvers centered on the company or "subdivision." While the 1764 Regulations prescribed specific arrangements for the deployment of companies based on seniority, in the field as a practical procedure companies were deployed as need arose without regard to the regulations.

In 1774 Major-General William Howe developed an experimental drill for a composite light battalion, which prescribed three different open-order formations. Normal "order" stipulated a separation of 2ft between men, while open order expanded that distance to 4ft and extended order required a 10ft separation. In June 1775 Major-General Thomas Gage ordered

British troops to operate in two-rank lines, but retained close order. While this formation enabled the men of the third rank to be engaged, it also proved difficult to maintain order when advancing across the numerous walls and fences that characterized the American battlefields. In February 1776 Howe ordered "regiments when formed by companies in battalions, or when on the general parade, are always to have their files 18 inches distant from one each other, which they will take care to practise in the future, being the order in which they are to engage the enemy" (quoted in Howe 1890: 222). Howe later amended the order, in May 1776 during the training at Halifax, ordering the grenadiers and line battalions back into a three-rank line but retaining the 18in distance between files, although this decision proved temporary. On August 1, 1776 Howe stipulated a two-rank line, with 18in distance between files, for the entire army. On assuming command in 1778 Lieutenant-General Sir Henry Clinton retained the two-rank, open-file formation for expediency's sake despite serious misgivings. Noting that it had worked well for the British, in part due to the lack of a threat from American cavalry, and that the Americans themselves had adopted it, he gave grudging approval for its continued use.

The British adopted three distinct speeds of movement on the battlefield. The "ordinary" speed of 75 paces per minute was used on parade and when moving over rough ground in line. "Quick time," requiring 120–150 paces per minute, was used for maneuvering or gaining ground. The fastest pace, the equivalent of a run, was used for bayonet charges. With the general use of the open order, two-line formation, combined with practical experience in combat, British commanders tended to rely on the quick time pace as a standard. When moving at the faster pace the British also adjusted the manner they carried their muskets. Normal practice for supporting the weapon was on the shoulder, which made rapid movement difficult. The alternative method, "trailed arms," required soldiers to grasp the middle of the musket with their right hand and extend their arm at their side.

American

Training was always a challenge for American troops given the uneven terms of enlistment and lack of prior formal military training of both men and officers. Diligent individual unit commanders drilled their men as opportunities allowed but the training was by no means uniform. Units almost never trained or maneuvered together, in part due to the fluid nature of the organization of the American Army, which moved units from brigades and division as events dictated. Even early in the war America units were drilled in rudimentary fire doctrine … or attempted to be. Joseph Plumb Martin described how, in early 1776, his regiment "attempted to fire by platoons for improvement, but we made blundering work of it; it was more like a running fire than firing by divisions" (quoted in Martin 1993: 28).

Early in the war the Americans attempted to implement the British 1764 Regulations or variations but found these cumbersome for the largely untrained recruits. Although some units performed well at the battles of Brandywine and Germantown the American Army still lacked the confidence to meet the British on the field of battle. During the winter of 1777–78 Frederick William Baron von Steuben joined the American army at Valley Forge and initiated a simpler training program. Steuben organized and trained a model company to serve as the nucleus of a broader training regime. During this period Steuben wrote the *Regulations for the Order and Discipline of the Troops of the United States.* Joseph Plumb Martin later wrote: "After I joined my regiment I was kept constantly, when off other duty, engaged in learning the Baron de Steuben's new Prussian exercise. It was a continual drill" (quoted in Martin 1993: 118).

This artwork shows a 26-year-old veteran of the campaigns around New York in 1776 as he advances in pursuit of the retreating Americans late in the day at Brandywine, after a grueling early-morning 12-mile march.

Weapons, dress, and equipment

This soldier carries a Brown Bess musket, 58½in long and outfitted with an 18in bayonet (**1**). A white leather sling (**2**) is attached to the underside of the musket. He wears a black felt hat (**3**) turned up on three sides and adorned with a black cockade; the top edge of the hat is bordered with white tape. He wears a white linen shirt (**4**) under his red coat, secured around his neck by a black stock (**5**). The stock was intended to hide dirt on the shirt and give a more uniform appearance. His coat (**6**) is made of wool, with black facing (**7**) along the collar, cuffs, and lapels. The lower portion of the coat is turned back and secured, showing the white lining of the coat (**8**). The facings are adorned with red, white, and black lace unique to the 64th Regiment, each buttonhole half an inch wide and accompanied by a pewter button (**9**). The lace is also applied to the lower back of the coat and side pockets.The soldier wears a linen waistcoat (**10**) and white woolen pants (**11**), secured just below the knee by the

buttons. He wears stockings made of yarn (**12**) and short gaiters (**13**). His leather shoes (**14**) could be worn on either foot.

His black leather cartridge box (**15**) features a regimental badge, backed in red cloth. The badge, made of heavy brass, was intended to weigh down the flap to prevent the accidental spilling of the cartridges. The cartridge box is slung across his shoulder with a 2¾in-wide buff leather belt (**16**) held in place by a shoulder strap buttoned near his collar. The bayonet scabbard (**17**) is also slung across his chest by a whitened buff leather belt. Attached to the bayonet belt is a brass plate engraved with the regimental device (**18**). A linen haversack holding additional cartridges and provisions is worn on his left side (**19**). The GR device signifies Crown ownership. Positioned on top of the haversack is a tin canteen, secured by a rope and slung over his shoulder (**20**). Altogether, these items of clothing, weaponry, and equipment equated to a combat load of about 35lbs.

CONDUCT IN BATTLE

Higher formations

For both sides individual regiments were organized as circumstances dictated into brigades. For the British these brigades could include three or four regiments, under the command of a brigadier-general, and operate as part of a division, which could include two to three brigades. In some theaters in which the size of the armies was small, brigades might represent the highest level of organization and be expected to operate independently. The American army was organized along similar lines, although a brigade could include four or five regiments depending on the depleted size of individual regiments.

Manoeuvre

Major Carl Baurmeister, Hessian adjutant general, noted soon after landing in America that:

> … these woods … are thickly grown with large trees and are full of gullies and ravines, which make it impossible for even three men to walk abreast, not to mention a platoon. Hence we were compelled to follow the example of the English, that is, to form in columns, two men abreast and rather far apart, as if lined up for some to run the gauntlet. (Baurmeister 1957: 36)

The unique character of the American countryside was just one of the factors that influenced the evolution of tactical doctrine for both sides during the Revolutionary War. By the end of the conflict experience had taught both British and American commanders that tactical flexibility was paramount. Although the light troops continued to operate in open-order, two-rank lines as the war continued British tactical doctrine, influenced by the increasing steadiness of their opponents and the influx of large numbers of replacements,

An engraving published in 1858 showing Friedrich Wilhelm Ludolf Gerhard Augustin, Baron von Steuben (1730–94). During early 1778 Baron von Steuben instituted a rigorous training program for the American Continentals, drilling them in linear tactics and instilling greater confidence in their ability to challenge the British. Despite lackluster command the American units trained by Steuben performed well at Monmouth. (ASKB)

These diagrams, showing the deployment of a regiment into line and related evolutions, were published in 1794 but were based on the regulations formalized by Steuben in 1778 and 1779. (ASKB)

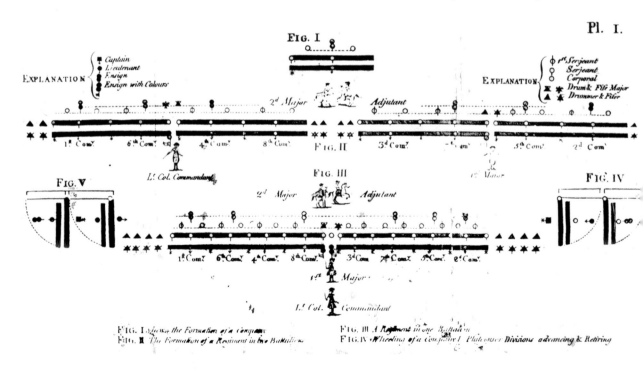

Pl. I.

began to shift back to more compact formations. British doctrine also evolved towards a tactical formation that allowed for the open-order formation to be used for the first line but that line was backed up by a second line in closed-order, three-rank line.

In early 1781 British troops operating in Virginia under the command of Major-General William Phillips, a veteran of the Seven Years War and Lieutenant-General John Burgoyne's Saratoga campaign, were instructed:

> Gen. Phillips gave out the following orders for exercising the troops, preparatory to their taking the field: "It is the Major General's wish, that the troops under his command may practise forming from two to three to four deep; and that they should be accustomed to charge in all those orders. In the latter orders, of the three and four deep, the files will, in course, be closer, so as to render the charge of the greatest force … The Major General would approve also of one division of a battalion attacking in the common open order of two deep, to be supported by the other compact division as a second line, in a charging order of three or four deep." (Simcoe 1844: 187–88)

During this same period, late in the war, American commanders also modified their tactical approach to fit specific circumstances. At the battle of Green Springs on July 6, 1781 the American advance "… drove in the enemy's pickets, marching at this time by companies, in open order …When perhaps within one hundred and fifty yards of the enemy we closed column and displayed; advanced in battalion until the firing commenced, and ran along the whole line" (Hunt 1892: 36–37).

Lieutenant Colonel John Mercer, who fought at Brandywine and Monmouth Courthouse, was critical of Major General Anthony Wayne's use of a close-order formation at Green Springs:

British musicians, 1775. Musicians played a critical role in the armies of both sides during the Revolutionary War. For British regiments each company was authorized two drummers, while grenadier companies were also allowed two fifers. In light companies the musicians employed horns while Highland companies included bagpipes. While the primary purpose of the musicians was to transmit orders there was a growing sense during the conflict that their effectiveness in that role was comprised by the noise and confusion of the battlefield. During the approach to combat musicians were used to control the evolution of units. (ASKB)

American battlefields dictated new approaches to tactics for both sides. Even relatively flat terrain could pose problems for the attacker. At Cowpens, for example, the American second line, composed of militia units, was deployed just beyond the crest of a slight rise, up which the British advanced. Hidden from view until the enemy crested the rise formed by the line of trees in the distance, the militia allowed the riflemen from the first line to retire through their ranks. (Author)

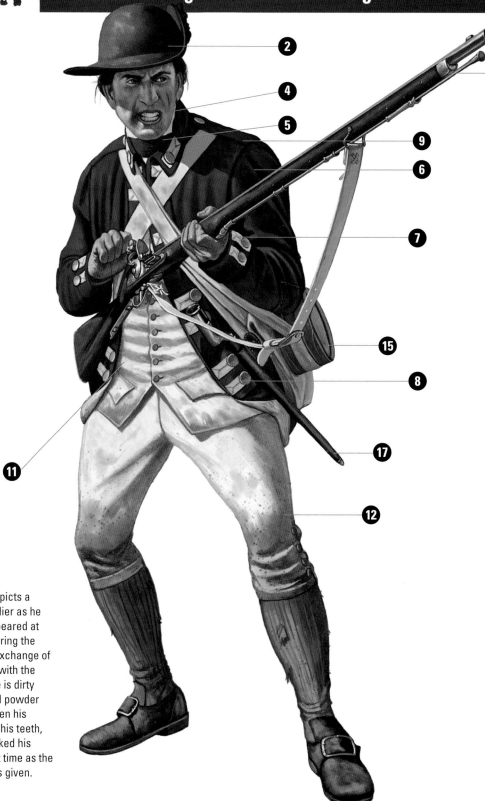

This artwork depicts a 22-year-old soldier as he would have appeared at Brandywine, during the early-evening exchange of musket volleys with the enemy. His face is dirty from smoke and powder after tearing open his cartridges with his teeth, and he has cocked his musket one last time as the order to retire is given.

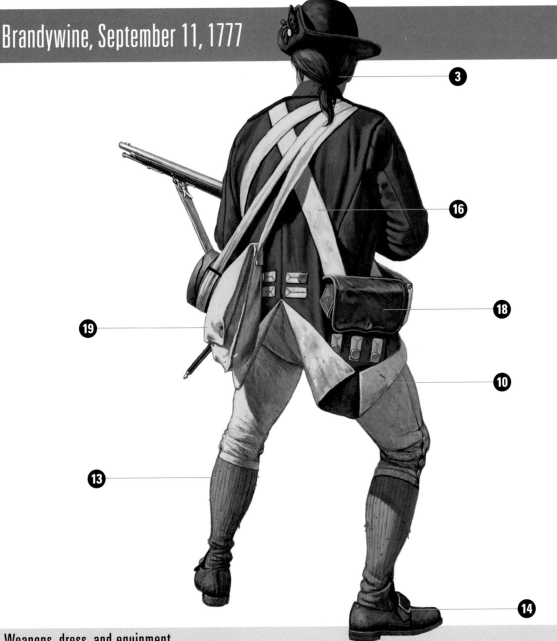

3

16

18

19

10

13

14

Weapons, dress, and equipment

The 2nd Virginia private carries a British Brown Bess musket (**1**), weighing approximately 10½lb, which was widely used by Continental forces until shipments of the French Charleville arrived in greater numbers. He wears a round hat (**2**) turned up on the left side and held in place with a black cockade. His hair is pulled back and tied in the back (**3**). He also wears a white shirt (**4**) with a black neck stock visible under his coat (**5**). The men of the 2nd Virginia were issued new uniforms in 1777 which featured dark blue coats (**6**) and facings with white worsted tape for lace (**7**). The lace pattern, unique to the 2nd Virginia, is composed of widely separated sets of two lace/button combinations on a blue facing on the cuffs and lapels (**8**) and a single lace/button on the blue collar. The coat includes straps (**9**) on both shoulders, attached with buttons and used to secure the cross belts. The tails of the coat are turned back and hooked together,

exposing the white lining of the coat (**10**). He wears a white waistcoat (**11**) and woolen pants (**12**). As the war progressed many units adopted overalls rather than pants, which were more practical and required replacement less often. Knee-high stockings (**13**) protected the soldier's calves while shoes (**14**), with brass buckles, completed the uniform. Slung at his side by a woven strap is a wooden canteen (**15**), sometimes painted in various colors or adorned with a regimental designation. Also supported by whitened buff leather crossbelts (**16**) are a leather bayonet scabbard (**17**) containing an 18in-long bayonet and a cartridge box (**18**), also made of leather and containing a wooden block drilled with 19 holes to hold the cartridges. He also carries a linen haversack (**19**) in which he may carry additional cartridges, food, or extra clothing. The combined weight of these items was roughly 35lbs.

We had just begun to assume the stiff German tactics, as the British acquir'd the good sense, from experience in our woody country, to lay it aside. Gen'l Wayne's Brigade were drawn up in such close order as to render it utterly impractical to advance inline and preserve their order – the line was necessarily broken by trees as they pass'd the wood.

The British advanc'd in open order at arm's length and aiming very low kept up a deadly fire. In this situation Gen'l Wayne gave repeated orders for the line to charge, but this operation was really impossible from the manner in which they were form'd and they could not push forward … (Quoted in Hunt 1892: 50)

Fire

Musket fire was governed, in theory, by the general regulations, which stipulated volleys were to be delivered in succession by fire divisions, which could include the four grand divisions, eight subdivisions, or 16 platoons in a predetermined sequence. The practice during the Revolutionary War appears more focused on delivering a single volley prior to a bayonet charge. This was not always possible given the broken nature of the terrain.

Several factors affected the accuracy of massed fire. The stress of combat, and the extra weight and difficulty of loading when the bayonet was attached, combined with a reluctance to aim along the barrel due to flaring from touchhole and kickback, conspired to diminish accuracy. Accuracy was also affected by the number of volleys due to accumulation of carbon deposits, heating of the barrel, and failure of flints. The use of the open- or extended-order formation in conjunction with the two-rank line tended to further diminish fire effectiveness.

Like many other things the experience and training of troops largely dictated whether that fire disciple could be maintained. Lieutenant Richard Williams of the 23rd Regiment noted that "the hurry and inattention natural to young troops; most of our regiment being composed of recruits and drafts, who, never having seen service, foolishly imagine that

A painting of the battle of Lexington (April 19, 1775) by William Barnes Wollen (1857–1936). Courtesy of the Council, National Army Museum, London, UK. The disposition of the British troops and American colonists in the painting represents the prevailing image of closely ranked British engaging a loosely formed enemy. The colonists were drawn up in a formal line on the village green at Lexington where, after refusing to disperse, they were fired upon by British regulars deployed in a three-rank, close-order formation. While some of the colonists that engaged in the running battle with the British on April 19, 1775 may have been veterans of the French and Indian War, they had little organization or training. After that initial exchange of musketry the American tactics largely involved hit-and-run attacks on the British column returning to Boston. The Colonists made extensive use of available cover, stone walls, and fences, and repeatedly forced the British to deploy from march column into line, only to find the Americans had dispersed. (Hulton Archive/Getty Images)

when danger is feared they secure themselves by discharging their muskets, with or without aim … Theory is nothing but practice, and it required one campaign, at least, to make a good soldier" (Williams 1954: 21–22). Due to the dispersed nature of the British formations the ability of officers and sergeants to maintain fire discipline was limited, leading to the men resorting to firing at will after the first disciplined volley.

This modern artwork by Domenick D'Andrea shows the Delaware Regiment deployed in a typical firing line at the battle of Long Island (August 27, 1776). (Public domain)

Close combat

No other factor tended to separate the abilities of the Americans and British as the use of the bayonet. British tactical doctrine stressed that volley fire should be controlled and limited, prefacing a decisive charge with the bayonet. Early in the war British troops could always disperse American units, whether riflemen in loose formation or Continentals in close order,

This British socket bayonet for Land Pattern muskets is of the standard type used by both sides throughout the Revolutionary War. (Image courtesy of the Military & Historical Image Bank)

A depiction of the battle of Bunker Hill (June 17, 1775) by Edward Percy Moran (1862–1935). Although the uniform details are inaccurate, the formation of the British grenadiers advancing uphill toward the Americans behind prepared positions is largely representative of the close-order formation used by the British during their assault. After the experience of the retreat from Lexington, British commander Lieutenant-General Thomas Gage ordered his men to form in two rather than three ranks but retained the close-order formation. Although Gage attempted to outflank the American position, a quick reaction by American commanders frustrated British efforts and resulted in a sustained firefight on unequal terms. The British grenadiers were ordered to assault the American lines with the bayonet but their close-order formations made it difficult for them to cross several fences and as the formations lost cohesion the grenadiers lost momentum. As a result many grenadiers began to fire at the enemy rather than carry home their charge. In the aftermath of Bunker Hill British commanders understood that the bayonet was the most effective weapon against the untrained Americans. Conversely, American commanders realized that effective use of terrain and cover, including walls, fences, and woods, could negate some of the lethal nature of the British bayonet charge. (Library of Congress)

with a bayonet charge. As the quality of American Continentals improved and they became more confident using bayonets, the British advantage diminished but did not disappear. The bayonet continued to be an effective tool, particularly when employed against riflemen or poorly trained militia.

British commanders struggled throughout the war to reinforce the need to fire a limited number of coordinated volleys before initiating the charge. The tendency for troops in combat, particularly new recruits or poorly trained units, was to engage in extended firefights. Lieutenant-General John Burgoyne was so distressed at the British performance at the battle of Freeman's Farm he issued a general order on September 21, 1777, stating:

> the impetuosity and uncertain aim of the British troops in giving their fire, and the mistake they are still under in preferring it to the bayonet, is much to be lamented. The Lieutenant General is persuaded that this error will be corrected in their next engagement, upon the conviction of their own reason and reflection, as well as upon that general precept of discipline, never to fire but by an order of an officer. (Quoted in Burgoyne 1780: 25)

Despite the relative success British bayonet charges enjoyed over their American opponents there were limits to its use. Responding to the premise that all British troops had to do to drive off American units was to charge with bayonets, former Major Edward Drewe of the 35th Regiment of Foot, writing after the war, published a series of satirical essays based on his experience. Drewe wrote: "Conceive the horrors of these [British] soldiers who, in our usual exhausted state, should come up with an enemy who stood firm and charged in their turn, fresh and in regular order?" (Drewe 1786: 74).

Brandywine

September 11, 1777

BACKGROUND TO BATTLE

The British campaign intended to capture the American capital of Philadelphia began on July 23, 1777 with the sailing from New York of a British force led by Lieutenant-General Sir William Howe. The ensuing weeks would see much uncertainty among Washington's men about the destination of the British force, with most believing Howe had sailed south toward South Carolina. Washington's army, numbering approximately 16,000, had been repositioning since the initial reports of the British sailing. Realizing the fatigue his men would endure marching in the late-summer heat, Washington endeavored to remain at Neshaminy Creek, 25 miles outside of Philadelphia, until British intentions became clear. On August 21 Washington held a council among his senior officers and there was agreement that given the continued lack of news the army should march north, either to confront Major-General John Burgoyne's invasion from Canada or even to attack New York. Orders were issued to march early on August 22 but news arrived during the day that the British fleet had been sighted in the Chesapeake Bay and were lately concentrated near Head of Elk, Maryland.

On August 25 the British fleet began disembarking the army at Turkey Point, 8 miles below Head of Elk. After the month-long sea voyage the British army was debilitated and in desperate need of resupply. Howe spent the next several days resting and reorganizing his army before setting out on August 28 toward Head of Elk. During this period Washington, with the divisions of Major General Nathanael Greene and Major General Adam Stephen, moved to Wilmington, Delaware and spent the next several days observing the British army while the scattered elements of the American army marched to join the main force. Following an American reverse at Cooch's Bridge on September 3,

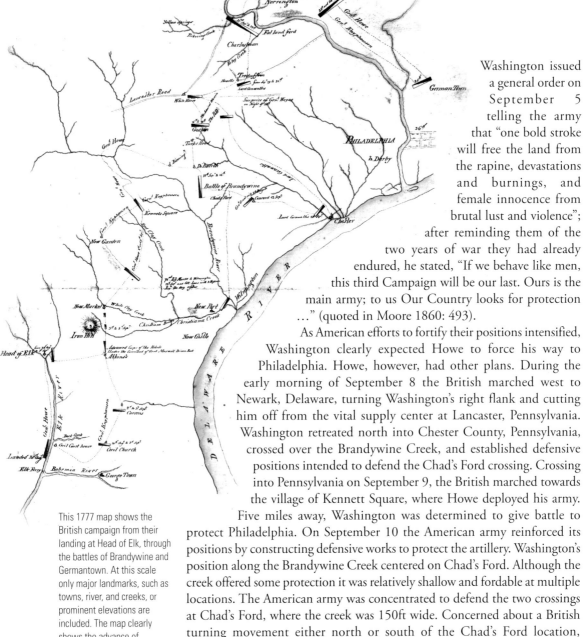

This 1777 map shows the British campaign from their landing at Head of Elk, through the battles of Brandywine and Germantown. At this scale only major landmarks, such as towns, river, and creeks, or prominent elevations are included. The map clearly shows the advance of Lieutenant-General Knyphausen against Chad's Ford and the wide flanking movement of Lieutenant-General Howe. It should be noted that the movements included on the map track British movement through September 25, 1777, just prior to their entry into Philadelphia. While the map includes the location of Germantown, the battle there did not take place until several weeks after the British occupation. (Library of Congress)

Washington issued a general order on September 5 telling the army that "one bold stroke will free the land from the rapine, devastations and burnings, and female innocence from brutal lust and violence"; after reminding them of the two years of war they had already endured, he stated, "If we behave like men, this third Campaign will be our last. Ours is the main army; to us Our Country looks for protection …" (quoted in Moore 1860: 493).

As American efforts to fortify their positions intensified, Washington clearly expected Howe to force his way to Philadelphia. Howe, however, had other plans. During the early morning of September 8 the British marched west to Newark, Delaware, turning Washington's right flank and cutting him off from the vital supply center at Lancaster, Pennsylvania. Washington retreated north into Chester County, Pennsylvania, crossed over the Brandywine Creek, and established defensive positions intended to defend the Chad's Ford crossing. Crossing into Pennsylvania on September 9, the British marched towards the village of Kennett Square, where Howe deployed his army.

Five miles away, Washington was determined to give battle to protect Philadelphia. On September 10 the American army reinforced its positions by constructing defensive works to protect the artillery. Washington's position along the Brandywine Creek centered on Chad's Ford. Although the creek offered some protection it was relatively shallow and fordable at multiple locations. The American army was concentrated to defend the two crossings at Chad's Ford, where the creek was 150ft wide. Concerned about a British turning movement either north or south of the Chad's Ford location, Washington deployed his army in a manner designed either to defend Chad's Ford or maneuver in response to a British flank march. As a result Washington's army was strung out over 5 miles to protect eight potential points of crossing the Brandywine Creek.

At Chad's Ford Washington deployed Brigadier General Anthony Wayne's division 200yd from the crossing. To the west of Chad's Ford, Brigadier General William Maxwell's newly formed light corps of 1,000 men was assigned to resist the British advance from Kennett Square. Several reinforced artillery positions were prepared to cover Chad's Ford. Supporting Wayne on the left were Greene's division and Brigadier General Francis Nash's North Carolina Brigade. A mile farther south, Major General John Armstrong covered Pyle's and Gibson's fords with 2,000 Pennsylvania militia. To the right of Wayne's command Major General William Alexander, Lord Stirling's division was deployed.

The battle of Brandywine would be fought over a series of rolling hills, interspersed with farms and heavily wooded areas. This view from Birmingham Hill towards Osborne's Hill illustrates the terrain the British and Hessians marched across to engage the Americans. The area along the Brandywine Creek is characterized by a series of hills rising above the numerous creeks. *Jäger* Captain Johann Ewald wrote that "this region of Pennsylvania is extremely mountainous and traversed by thick forests; nevertheless it is very well cultivated and very fertile" (Ewald 1979: 79). New England soldier Elkannah Watson marched through the area in 1778 and noted that "most of the slopes of the hill-sides are laid out into regular farms, and under high cultivation. The verdue of the fields, and the neatness and superior tillage of the farms in the rich vales, were so graceful to the eye …" (Watson 1856: 62). From high points it was possible to see some distance, but the woods obscured even large formations of men. The British could only see a portion of the American deployment of Stirling and Stephen's divisions from Osborne's Hill and Major General Sullivan was initially unable to see Stirling's division deployed a half-mile to his right. (Author)

To Stirling's right was Stephen's division. Brigadier General John Sullivan's division was assigned to protect the Brinton Ford, 1 mile north of Chad's Ford. From Sullivan's division Colonel David Hall's Delaware Continental Regiment was detached to guard Jones' Ford, 1 mile from Brinton, and Colonel Moses Hazen's 2nd Canadian Regiment was assigned to watch the Wister Ford and Buffington's Ford. Beyond Buffington's Ford Colonel Theodorick Bland's 1st Light Cavalry Regiment patrolled both sides of the Brandywine. Apparently unknown to Washington or other American officers was the existence of additional fords beyond Buffington's.

Howe, for his part, intended to repeat the flanking maneuver that he had used to such great effect in the campaign around New York in 1776, to attack the American army. Howe recognized the strength of his better-trained force was in their ability to fight a battle of maneuver. Conversely, the strength of the less-experienced American soldiers was their tenacity when defending fixed positions such as the ones Washington prepared as part of his defense of the Brandywine crossings. On the morning of September 11 Howe divided his army, assigning approximately 5,000 men under Lieutenant-General Baron Wilhelm Knyphausen to advance towards Chad's Ford while he accompanied Major-General Earl Charles Cornwallis with the flanking column of 8,200 men. Knyphausen's task was to demonstrate at Chad's Ford, giving Washington the impression that the British were attempting to force their way across the creek and encourage the American commander to redeploy his forces to resist the attack over the ford.

While Knyphausen fixed Washington's attention to his front, Howe and Cornwallis would march along the Great Valley Road around the American right flank and cross the Brandywine Creek. Guided by local Loyalists, Howe intended to march beyond Buffington's Ford, cross the West Branch of the Brandywine at Trimble's Ford and then the East Branch at Jeffries' Ford before descending on the American flank. The strategy was not without risk. If Washington discovered Howe's march he could launch an attack on Knyphausen's isolated command and defeat him in detail before Howe reached his crossing point. With Knyphausen defeated it would be Howe's column that would be in danger.

MAP KEY

1 **1415hrs:** General Washington receives Colonel Bland's note and immediately orders Stirling's and Stephen's divisions to march north to the Birmingham Meetinghouse. He also orders Sullivan to advance his division north and assume overall command of Stirling's and Stephen's divisions.

2 **1430hrs:** Sullivan receives the order from Washington.

3 **1500hrs:** The British advance guard moves south from Osborne Hill towards the Street Road. The 3rd Virginia defends the orchard against *Jäger* and British light infantry.

4 **1515hrs:** Sullivan's division deploys on high ground south of the Street Road.

5 **1530hrs:** *Jäger* and British light infantry engage the 3rd Virginia at the Birmingham Meetinghouse.

6 **1545hrs:** Sullivan confers with Stephen and Stirling and agrees to move his division east.

7 **1600hrs:** Stephen and Stirling shift to the east, leaving a 300yd gap between their formations.

8 **1615hrs:** The 3rd Virginia abandons the Birmingham Meetinghouse and retires to the main line of Stephen's division.

9 **1630hrs:** The Guards Brigade advances against Sullivan's division, which is in the process of redeploying.

10 **1645hrs:** British grenadiers approach Stirling's division.

11 **1650hrs:** Sullivan's division scatters.

12 **1700hrs:** Washington orders Greene's division to withdraw from Chad's Ford to support Sullivan.

13 **1700hrs:** Stirling's division engages in a firefight with the British grenadiers and is pushed back from its positions.

14 **1715hrs:** Knyphausen launches an attack on the American defenders of Chad's Ford.

15 **1725hrs:** Stirling's division fails to counterattack and retreats. The Marquis de Lafayette joins Brigadier General Thomas Conway's brigade but fails to rally them and is wounded.

16 **1730hrs:** The 2nd Light Infantry Battalion, supported by Brigadier-General James Agnew's 4th Brigade, assaults Stephen's division at Sandy Hollow.

17 **1745hrs:** Stephen's division retreats and the 1st Light Infantry Battalion overruns the American battery.

18 **1800hrs:** Washington and his headquarters unit arrive at Dilworth as elements of Sullivan's line retreat through the village.

19 **1815hrs:** Sunset; Brigadier General George Weedon's 2nd Virginia Brigade arrives southwest of Dilworth.

20 **1820hrs:** The British halt their advance at Dilworth to re-form.

21 **1830hrs:** Sullivan's line is in full retreat. Weedon's brigade is deployed east of the Wilmington Road.

22 **1900hrs:** The 2nd Grenadier Battalion advances east of the Wilmington Road and is taken under fire by Weedon's brigade deployed along a fence line and in adjacent woods. Colonel Henry Monckton, the 2nd Grenadier Battalion commander, requests reinforcements.

23 **1925hrs:** Agnew directs his 4th Brigade to support Monckton's grenadiers. The 46th and 64th regiments advance on the left of the grenadiers. The 64th Regiment engages in a prolonged firefight with Weedon's brigade deployed to the 64th Regiment's front and along the left flank.

24 **1945hrs:** The British deploy two 12-pdr cannon and drive Weedon's men out of the wooded area on the 64th Regiment's left flank.

25 **2000hrs:** The battle ends as Weedon's brigade retires.

Battlefield environment

While the area east of the Brandywine Creek was dotted with farmsteads and large estates, interspersed with stands of thick forest, the area along the creek was rocky and covered with woods. The movement of the armies into the Brandywine Valley found the local farmers preparing to plant winter wheat in late September and harvest their crop of buckwheat in early October. Fields of barley, oats, and Indian corn also dotted the landscape along with orchards laden with apples and peaches. Fields were marked by split-rail fences or sturdier stone walls, making cross-country movement difficult for formed troops. A lack of appreciable rainfall since late August had left the ground dry and hard and the creeks shrunken and narrow.

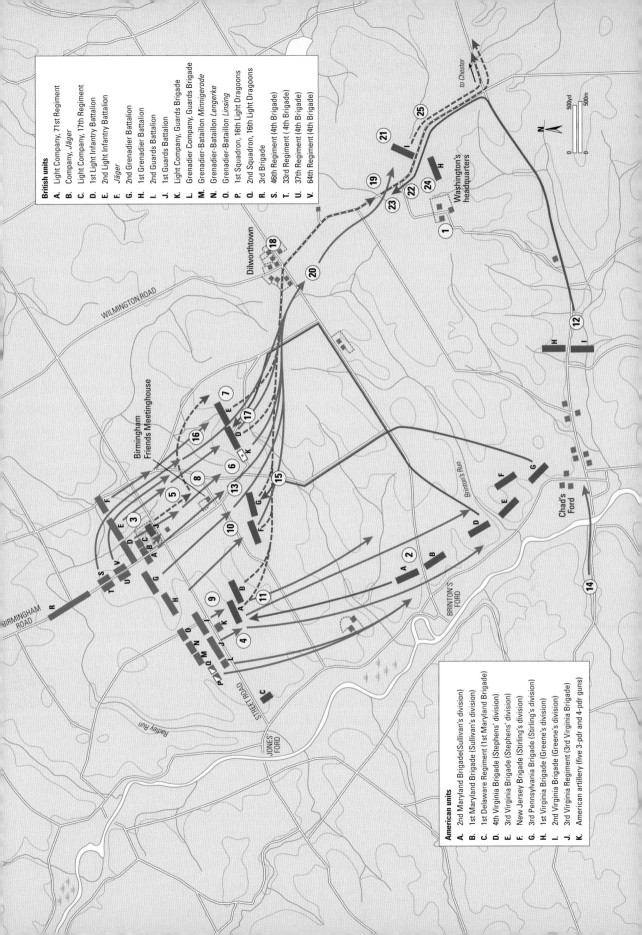

British units

A. Light Company, 71st Regiment
B. Company, *Jäger*
C. Light Company, 17th Regiment
D. 1st Light Infantry Battalion
E. 2nd Light Infantry Battalion
F. *Jäger*
G. 2nd Grenadier Battalion
H. 1st Grenadier Battalion
I. 2nd Guards Battalion
J. 1st Guards Battalion
K. Light Company, Guards Brigade
L. Grenadier Company, Guards Brigade
M. Grenadier-Bataillon *Minnigerode*
N. Grenadier-Bataillon *Lengerke*
O. Grenadier-Bataillon *Linsing*
P. 1st Squadron, 16th Light Dragoons
Q. 2nd Squadron, 16th Light Dragoons
R. 3rd Brigade
S. 46th Regiment (4th Brigade)
T. 33rd Regiment (4th Brigade)
U. 37th Regiment (4th Brigade)
V. 64th Regiment (4th Brigade)

American units

A. 2nd Maryland Brigade(Sullivan's division)
B. 1st Maryland Brigade (Sullivan's division)
C. 1st Delaware Regiment (1st Maryland Brigade)
D. 4th Virginia Brigade (Stephens' division)
E. 3rd Virginia Brigade (Stephens' division)
F. New Jersey Brigade (Stirling's division)
G. 3rd Pennsylvania Brigade (Stirling's division)
H. 1st Virginia Brigade (Greene's division)
I. 2nd Virginia Brigade (Greene's division)
J. 3rd Virginia Regiment (3rd Virginia Brigade)
K. American artillery (five 3-pdr and 4-pdr guns)

Major-General Sir William Howe (1729–1814) is depicted in this painting by Richard Purcell published in 1777. Before returning to North America in March 1775, Howe had seen long service. After fighting in Europe during the Seven Years' War, Howe played a key role in the capture of Quebec in 1759 and the subsequent campaign against the French. After criticizing Lieutenant-General Thomas Gage over tactics at Bunker Hill in June 1775, Howe was eventually given overall command that September. Under Howe's leadership the British landed on Staten Island in July 1776 and during the fall of 1776 outmaneuvered General George Washington at Long Island and New York, forcing the Americans to retreat in disorder across New Jersey. During the Fall campaign Howe clashed with both Major-General Charles Cornwallis and Major-General Henry Clinton over strategy. Washington's victory at Trenton revived American spirits and during 1777 Howe endeavored to regain the initiative by capturing the American capital at Philadelphia. Although this was successful, Howe's failure to coordinate his movements with Major General John Burgoyne's invasion from Canada resulted in Burgoyne's surrender. (ASKB)

INTO COMBAT

September 11, 1777 dawned grey with a heavy mist that covered the valleys and hollows but burned off by the late morning, replaced by bright late-summer sun. Marching under a thick fog, which provided some hope of masking their movements, Howe and Cornwallis set out at 0500hrs from the Marlborough Friends Meetinghouse, 3 miles from Kennett Square. At about 0600hrs the leading elements of Knyphausen's column clashed with Maxwell's outposts at Welch's Tavern. From that point the American light infantry and riflemen engaged the British advance force in a running battle lasting nearly two hours, while the Americans slowly retired towards Chad's Ford. As Maxwell fed more troops into the fight and American resistance stiffened, Knyphausen brought up additional troops; by 1030hrs he had formed a line along the heights west of the Brandywine and by 1100hrs all of Maxwell's men had been driven across the creek. For the next few hours Knyphausen kept up a steady fire, while British units feigned withdrawal to goad Maxwell's men to cross the creek into preplanned ambushes.

While Washington's attention was focused on Knyphausen's advance, he continued to receive sporadic reports from his forces protecting the upper fords. Although Knyphausen's advance was troubling, Washington was wary of the possibility that Howe would attempt to turn his flank. Various reports filtered back to Washington about British movements throughout the morning. At mid-morning a patrol from the 7th Maryland Regiment (Sullivan's division) stopped at a farm overlooking Trimble's Ford, 4 miles from Brinton's Ford, and watched as the head of Cornwallis's column came into view about a mile to the south. At some point between 1000hrs and 1100hrs Howe's men began crossing Trimble's Ford. At 1100hrs a patrol from Dunlap's Partizan Regiment, commanded by Lieutenant Colonel James Ross, tangled with British light infantry near Trimble's Ford and Ross scribbled a hurried note to Washington, alerting him to the presence of a large British force apparently headed for Jeffries' Ford. Washington received Ross's note sometime before 1200hrs.

Somewhat earlier in the morning, just after 1100hrs, Washington, desperate for information about British movements, sent a terse message to Colonel Bland of the light dragoons:

Sir: I earnestly entreat a continuance of your vigilant attention to the movements of the enemy, and the earliest report not only of their movements, but of their numbers and the course they are pursuing. In a particular manner I wish to gain satisfactory information of a body confidently reported to have gone up to a ford seven or eight miles above this. It is said the fact is certain. You will send up an intelligent, sensible officer immediately with a party to find out the truth, what number it consists of, and the road they are now on. Be particular in these matters. (Quoted in Reed 1847: 309)

Captain John Marshall of the 15th Virginia Regiment (Weedon's brigade, Greene's division) reported that

… information reached General Washington that a large column with many field pieces, had taken a road leading from Kennett's Square, directly up the country,

and had entered the great valley road, down which they were marching to the upper fords of the Brandywine. This information was given by Colonel Ross of Pennsylvania, who was in their rear, and estimated their numbers at five thousand men. (Quoted in Marshall 1925: 300)

After receiving Ross's report Washington decided to attack Knyphausen and ordered Maxwell, Sullivan, and Greene to cross the Brandywine. As preparations were being made Sullivan received reports from various militia patrols that no British troops had been seen on the Great Valley Road. Although skeptical of the information, Sullivan duly passed it along to Washington. Washington had by now finally heard from Bland, whose report only further confused the situation:

> Not long after the first communication was made by Colonel Ross, information was received from Colonel Bland of the cavalry, which produced some doubt respecting the strength of this column. He saw only two brigades; but the dust appeared to rise in their rear for a considerable distance. A major of the militia came in, who alleged that he left the forks of the Brandywine so late in the day that it was supposed Lord Cornwallis must have passed them by that time, had he continued his march in that direction, and who asserted that no enemy had appeared in that quarter. Some light horsemen who had been sent to reconnoiter the road, returned with the same information. (Quoted in Marshall 1925: 300–01)

Faced with uncertainty and the real possibility that the British column seen on the Great Valley Road might have changed course, Washington suspended the order to attack Knyphausen. While Washington vacillated, Howe pushed his column forward, reaching Jeffries' Ford at about 1200hrs. Surprised to find it unguarded, the British column quickly spilled over the creek and moved south to Strode's Mill. Detachments of Hazen's 2nd Canadian Regiment, guarding Buffington's and Wistar's fords just over 1 mile to the right of the British columns, were now some distance behind the British flank and in danger of being isolated. A mile south from Osborne's Hill was the Street

Movement across the Brandywine battlefield required crossing a series of fences like the one pictured here. These fences bordered most roadways and fields among the surrounding farms. Adding to obstacles to the movement of large formations of men were the small watercourses that fed the Brandywine Creek. Although a lack of rain rendered them largely dry, crossing these deep cuts disordered infantry formations and delayed the movement of artillery. Moreover, the woods of the Brandywine battlefield were accompanied by thick underbrush, making movement through them difficult and providing defenders with cover and screening their movement. (Author)

Road, which ran east to west and provided access to Jones' Ford where Hall's Delaware Regiment was deployed.

Just after 1300hrs Bland observed Hessian patrols on Osborne's Hill and sent a message to Washington and Sullivan. Upon receiving Bland's note, which confirmed his worst fears, Washington ordered Stephen and Stirling to move their divisions north to the Birmingham Meetinghouse and contest the British advance. He also ordered Sullivan to march his division to support Stephen and Stirling and take overall command. Sullivan reported receiving his orders at approximately 1430hrs and immediate set his men in motion. Stirling's division, deployed near Brinton's Ford, passed through the important crossroads at Dilworth and deployed along a ridge, Birmingham Hill, about a half-mile south of the Birmingham Meetinghouse. Stephen, following closely behind, deployed his men to the right of Stirling's. A battery of five light cannon, 3-pdr and 4-pdr guns, was positioned between the two divisions, covering the Birmingham Road coming south from Osborne's Hill. Sullivan directed his division north along the east side of the Brandywine Creek. In addition to employing this more direct route, Sullivan hoped to reunite his division with Hall's Delaware Regiment and Hazen's 2nd Canadian Regiment on the way. From Osborne's Hill the British watched the Americans' deployment take shape. Behind the Hill Howe's men were resting, having marched more than 12 miles in eight hours.

As Sullivan moved north he met Hazen, who had watched the British cross Jeffries' Ford and reported to Sullivan that the strength of the British force appeared much higher than the two brigades reported earlier by Bland. Sullivan deployed his division on high ground south of the Street Road and observed Stirling and Stephen's men on Birmingham Hill about a half-mile from his position. Concerned about the gap in the American line, Sullivan rode over to confer with Stirling and Stephen. They agreed Sullivan should move to his right to close the gap as soon as possible. Rather than simply shifting to the right to tie in with Stirling's left flank, however, Brigadier General Philippe Hubert, Chevalier Preudhomme de Borre insisted that his 2nd Maryland Brigade, deployed on Sullivan's left, should have the traditional place of honor on the right. This threw Sullivan's division into confusion just as the British were beginning their advance and forced both Stirling's and Stephen's divisions to redeploy also. Placing the majority of his 3rd Virginia Brigade (Stephen's division) on a small hill 100yd behind the Birmingham Meetinghouse, Brigadier General William Woodford sought to protect his right flank by deploying the 170 men of Colonel Thomas Marshall's 3rd Virginia Regiment in an orchard north of the meetinghouse with "orders to hold the wood as long as it was tenable and then retreat to the right of the brigade" (Cecere 2007: 63). With the shift of the main body of Woodford's brigade the 3rd Virginia Regiment was left isolated in advance of the main American line. Brigadier General George Weedon, commander of the 2nd Virginia Brigade (Greene's division), later wrote that "in making this alteration, unfavorable Ground, made it necessary for Woodford to move his Brigade 200 paces back of the line & threw Marshall's wood in his front" (quoted in Cecere 2007: 63).

At 1500hrs the *Jäger* and British light infantry were ordered to move down from Osborne's Hill. By 1530hrs they were engaged with Marshall's men in the orchard. The Virginia Continentals forced the *Jäger* and light infantry to take cover behind a fence line and for 30 minutes they engaged in a furious firefight. While the British advance guard was skirmishing with Marshall's men the main British battle line was being organized. Brigadier-General Edward Mathew's Guards Brigade was assigned to advance on the right, while the two grenadier battalions formed the center. The two light-infantry battalions were assigned the left of the line and the *Jäger* were ordered to support the British light infantry by protecting their left flank. The three Hessian grenadier battalions were ordered to support the British Guards and grenadiers while Brigadier-General James Agnew's 4th Brigade was to support the light infantry. Brigadier-General James Grey's 3rd Brigade remained in reserve on Osborne's Hill.

At 1600hrs the British regimental bands struck up 'The British Grenadiers' and the main British attack was under way. Major John Maitland's 2nd Light Infantry Battalion led the advance followed by Lieutenant-Colonel Robert Abercromby's 1st Light Infantry Battalion. Both battalions deployed into extended order, Maitland's on the left and Abercromby's on the right. The grenadiers and Guards marched from the Birmingham Road to the right, deploying from column of march to open-order line as they moved forward. The advance of the British light infantry, supported by the *Jäger*, forced Marshall's 3rd Virginia Regiment out of the orchard. The Virginians retired 100yd to the walled cemetery of the Friends meetinghouse, where they kept up a continuous fire that forced the British units to incline to their right to avoid the stronghold.

In the center the 1st and 2nd Grenadier battalions, now wearing their bearskin hats, completed their deployment into line. Just after 1630hrs the grenadiers moved forward across Street Road and directly towards Stirling's and Stephen's divisions. Lieutenant William Hale of the 45th Regiment's Grenadier Company, part of the 2nd Grenadier Battalion, later wrote "nothing could be more dreadfully pleasing than the line moving on to the attack; the Grenadiers put on their Caps and struck up their march, believe me I would not exchange those three minutes of rapture to avoid ten thousand times the danger" (quoted in Wilkin 1914: 213). The American battery kept up an incessant fire as the American infantry waited in nervous silence. As Lieutenant Ebenezer Elmer of the 3rd New Jersey Regiment (Stirling's division) later wrote, "The Enemy Came on with fury" (Elmer 1911: 105). Opposite Sullivan's division, the Guards Brigade deployed and advanced.

Sullivan, who had remained in the center after conferring with Stirling and Stephen, watched as the British advanced. The shifting of the American line to the right was initiated as the British began their advance, adding to the sense of unease among the largely untrained and inexperienced Continentals deployed along Birmingham Hill. Sullivan's division was still completing its movement, including de Borre's ill-advised change of position, when the British Guards approached. Adding to the confusion, units of de Borre's brigade fired into the rear of the 1st Maryland Brigade (also Sullivan's division) deployed to their front. After firing several volleys Sullivan's division began to disintegrate.

In the center, Stirling's and Stephen's divisions maintained their positions. The American battery fire and the 3rd Virginia Regiment's defense of the meetinghouse had stymied the advance of the British light infantry for some time. As the British grenadiers advanced across Street Road, supported by several 6-pdr and 12-pdr guns, the Continentals directed their fire at bearskins to their front. The American artillery also targeted the advancing grenadiers, giving the British light infantry an opportunity to recover and creep forward. Stirling's two brigades, composed of Pennsylvania and New Jersey Continentals, held firm and engaged the grenadiers as they struggled to cross several fence lines. Dr. Lewis Howell of the New Jersey Brigade (Stirling's division) later wrote: "We had been there but a short time when they appeared, and the heaviest firing I ever heard began, continuing a long time, every inch of ground being disputed" (quoted in Agnew 1898: 224). Elmer recalled that "our men stood firing upon them most amazingly, killing almost all before them for an hour till they got within 6 rod [roughly 100ft] of each other ..." (Elmer 1911: 105).

Despite the loss of several officers – including Lieutenant-Colonel William Meadow, commander of the 1st Grenadier Battalion – the grenadiers coolly re-formed after crossing the fence lines and after receiving one last volley from the Continentals the British leveled their muskets and charged. Emboldened by the advance of the grenadiers and seeing the enemy wavering, the British light infantry rallied and charged, overrunning the American artillery battery. Stirling's men were driven back some distance by the grenadier charge. Sullivan and Stirling retired to a strong position atop a hill near Sandy Hollow, southeast of Birmingham Hill. American officers, aided by volunteer Marquis de Lafayette, tried in vain to organize a bayonet counterattack. Stirling's two brigades slowly retired, dispersing in the face of the British advance but rallying to re-form at the next fence line or ridge line.

As Stirling's retreat exposed their left flank the men of Stephen's division, defending Sandy Hollow, braced themselves for the British attack. Several companies of the 2nd Light Infantry Battalion, supported by the 33rd and 46th regiments (both 4th Brigade), engaged Stephen's men while *Jäger* worked their way around the American right flank. Lieutenant Martin Hunter of the 2nd Light Infantry Battalion described the stubborn American defense: "they stood the charge till we came to the last paling ... the Americans never fought so well before, and they fought to great advantage" (Hunter 1894: 29–30). As the troops on the left fell back, Woodford's 3rd Virginia Brigade remained on Birmingham Hill. The British brought up some artillery, firing into the American left flank. "Further in this sudden cannonade, Woodford was wounded and retired from the hill to have his wounds dressed" (Smith 1976: 19). With the British light infantry within 20yd, Woodford's brigade collapsed, retiring into the protection of the woods to the rear.

It was now 1830hrs and the late-summer sun began to cast angled light across the fields and through the woods. Following hard on the heels of the retreating Americans, the British line began to separate. At first the two battalions of the Guards Brigade moved in unison south from the Street Road but then the 1st Guards Battalion moved to the right, away from the 2nd Guards Battalion. The lengthening gap between the Guards and the grenadiers was filled by the Hessian grenadiers deployed directly to their rear, but the Germans' slow, deliberate marching delayed their movement.

Shortly after 1700hrs Washington had ordered Greene to withdraw his division and march to the support of Sullivan's force. Leaving Maxwell's, Wayne's, and Nash's commands to guard the Chad's Ford crossing, Washington moved north with Greene. Weedon's 2nd Virginia Brigade, composed of the 2nd, 6th, 10th, and 14th Virginia Regiments and Colonel Walter Stewart's Pennsylvania State Regiment, headed east and then north along the main road to the village of Dilworth. Knyphausen, recognizing Howe's engagement from the sound of cannon fire to the north, ordered an attack across the Brandywine. At 1715hrs, as Greene's division was withdrawing to the north, British troops crossed the Brandywine in the face of fire from Maxwell's light infantry and Colonel Thomas Proctor's

This 1909 painting by Edward Percy Moran (1862–1935) depicts Marquis de Lafayette's baptism of fire. Accompanying the American army at Brandywine as a volunteer, Lafayette rushed to help rally the men of Brigadier General Thomas Conway's 3rd Pennsylvania Brigade (Stirling's division). Despite his repeated attempts to organize a bayonet counterattack, the American troops were forced to retire and Lafayette was slightly wounded in the leg. (Library of Congress)

battery. Wayne's division held a line 500yd east of the ford; his entire line was soon heavily engaged by the British attack and retired, leaving all but two guns behind. Noticing British troops – men of the Guards Brigade, who had advanced south along the Brandywine after scattering Sullivan's division – filtering through the woods on the hills to his right and recognizing the vulnerability of his position as evening fell, Wayne ordered an immediate retirement to high ground 600yd to the east.

Meanwhile, Washington and his headquarters staff, which included Brigadier General Henry Knox and Count Casimir Pulaski, rode quickly towards Dilworth, arriving at 1800hrs near the edge of a field southwest of the village, where they found a confused scene. Continental soldiers, individually and as units, were streaming back out of the woods. Behind them the British grenadiers and light infantry moved through the smoke and haze in the late-afternoon light. Sundown on September 11, 1777 was approximately 1815hrs. Knox directed two cannon be deployed behind a fence on a small rise while the British halted their advance at the Birmingham Road, just west of Dilworth, to re-form and allow their artillery to catch up. The British quickly brought up several 12-pdr cannon, which drove the American artillery back 200yd to another fence line.

Weedon's men, moving at the trot, covered almost 4 miles in 45 minutes and arrived southeast of Dilworth just as Sullivan's men came streaming south from their defense of Birmingham Hill and Sandy Hollow. Colonel Charles Pinckney, serving in Washington's headquarters, was ordered by Sullivan to request that Weedon deploy Colonel Alexander Spottswood's 2nd Virginia Regiment and Colonel Edward Stevens' 10th Virginia Regiment in a ploughed field on the right. Weedon deployed his men 400yd east of the Wilmington Road, behind a small rise on which portions of Stirling's and Stephen's divisions had formed, along a fence line bordering a ploughed field. He extended his right flank along another fence line in a wooded area that ran at a 90-degree angle to his main line, forming an "L"-shaped formation.

James McMichael

James McMichael was a native of Scotland, emigrating to Lancaster County, Pennsylvania several years before the outbreak of war. McMichael entered service in April 1776, enlisting as a sergeant in the Pennsylvania Rifle Regiment. In March 1777 McMichael was promoted to 1st lieutenant in the Pennsylvania State Regiment. McMichael fought at Trenton in 1776 and at Princeton and Brandywine in 1777. The Pennsylvania State Regiment was part of Weedon's brigade and played a prominent role in the twilight battle with the British 2nd Grenadier Battalion and 64th Regiment.

The Pennsylvania State Regiment was placed on the Continental Establishment in November 1777 as the 13th Pennsylvania Regiment. McMichael spent the next several years serving in different Pennsylvania units including the 7th and 4th regiments before ending the war in 1783 assigned to the 1st Pennsylvania Regiment. He was mustered out of service in late 1783 and became a member of the Society of the Cincinnati, a Continental veterans' organization, in Pennsylvania in 1789. Several years later McMichael sailed to Scotland, but his ship was lost at sea.

OPPOSITE

A British infantryman – possibly of the 33rd Regiment of Foot, as suggested by his red facings – is shown in this undated watercolor. He appears to be performing movement 11 – "ram down your cartridge" – as prescribed in *The Manual Exercise* of 1764. The 33rd Regiment fought at Brandywine as part of the 4th Brigade. The 33rd and 64th regiments would be engaged in repulsing the American attack at Germantown on October 4, 1777. During that action Brigadier-General Agnew was killed. (ASKB)

In the gathering twilight the 2nd Grenadier Battalion, supported by the 4th Brigade, advanced towards the American line visible east of the Wilmington Road. As the British pushed through the disorganized remnants of Stirling's and Stephen's divisions they stumbled into the southernmost portion of Weedon's 2nd Virginia Brigade, drawn out in line. Grenadier Captain John Peebles of the 1st Grenadier Battalion related that "they came upon a second and more extensive line of the Enemy's best Troops drawn up and posted to great advantage, here they sustained a warm attack for some time & pour'd a heavy fire on the British Troops as they came up" (quoted in Gruber 1997: 133). Finding the American line standing firm Monckton, the 2nd Grenadier Battalion commander, ordered Hessian Captain Johann Ewald to ride back for reinforcements.

Lieutenant James McMichael of the Pennsylvania State Regiment (2nd Virginia Brigade) described the action at dusk: "we took the front and attacked the enemy, and being engaged with their grand army, we at first were obliged to retreat a few yards and formed in an open field, when we fought without giving way on either side until dark. Our ammunition almost expended firing ceased on both sides, when we received orders to proceed to Chester" (McMichael 1892: 150). Ewald quickly found 4th Brigade commander Brigadier-General James Agnew and requested assistance for the grenadiers, pointing out the small rise east of the Wilmington Road. Led by the 46th and 64th regiments, the men of the 4th Brigade trudged up and over the hill only to find themselves engaged on along their front and left flank by a strong line of Continentals. Ewald related that "at this point there was terrible firing, and half of the Englishmen and nearly all the officers of these two regiments were slain" (Ewald 1979: 86). The men of the British 64th Regiment, having marched since before dawn, were tired but focused on the enemy they could see through the gathering darkness arrayed in a silent line across the field. As they moved forward, urged on by their sergeants, they would have seen Agnew, accompanied by his staff, including Alexander Andrew, riding on their right, between them and the 46th Regiment.

Watching the British advance across the ploughed field, the soldiers of the 2nd Virginia Regiment, still recovering from their trot from Chad's Ford, looked about nervously. On their left the 10th Virginia Regiment and Pennsylvania State Regiment dressed their lines. The men of the 2nd Virginia Regiment noted the British seemed unaware that the 6th Virginia Regiment was deployed

Alexander Andrew

Persuaded into enlisting by his older brother William, then serving in the 44th Regiment of Foot, as a means of his own withdrawal from the army, Alexander Andrew – also a Scot – joined the 44th Regiment in 1772, aged 21. When the 44th sailed for America in early 1775, Andrew went as the personal servant to its commanding officer, Lieutenant-Colonel James Agnew. In March 1776 Agnew was promoted and given command of the 4th Brigade; as Agnew's servant, Andrew had access to better and more frequent food as well as lodging in the same house as Agnew when on campaign. Although grazed by a cannon ball during the dusk attack against Weedon's brigade, Agnew remained in command until the American withdrawal. At the battle of Germantown on October 4, 1777 Andrew again accompanied Agnew in battle; an American volley killed Agnew and wounded Andrew. Andrew returned to the ranks and was promoted to corporal in December 1777 and sergeant in October 1778. He accompanied the 44th Regiment to Canada in 1779, and retired from the regiment as a quartermaster-sergeant in 1793.

in the woodline, behind a fence, on the left of the advancing 64th Regiment. Even the soldiers of the 2nd Virginia Regiment couldn't see their sister regiment, which was hidden by the dense woods and lengthening shadows. Somewhere off to the left of the 2nd Virginia Regiment a cannon fired, the sound reverberating through the still twilight. Suddenly the men of the 2nd Virginia Regiment heard the command to make ready and some noted it seemed to echo down the line of the neighboring regiments. They also noticed movement in the woods on their right as men of the 6th Virginia Regiment stepped forward and took position along the fence.

Some of the 64th Regiment soldiers nearest the woods also became aware of the sudden movement on the left but they were more concerned with the firm stance of the American soldiers to their front. As the command to halt was shouted along the 64th Regiment's line, the American line erupted in deafening sound and a blaze of yellow and orange, followed by billowing smoke rising in the air. Ignoring the fallen dead and the cries of the wounded, the men of the 64th Regiment methodically performed the actions to load their muskets and on command fired a volley into the shadowy line before them while the sergeants struggled to fill the gaps and reorder the line. Although the 46th Regiment suffered minor casualties the 64th lost over 10 percent of its strength, suffering 47 casualties out of a total strength of 420 men, the highest loss of any British regiment during the battle. Captain John Montresor, Howe's Chief Engineer, wrote that "they poured out on us particularly on the Guards [*sic*; probably Grenadiers] and the 4th Brigade, the heaviest fire during the action" (quoted in Scull 1881: 450). Major General Sullivan later stated that "Weedon's Brigade was the only part of Greens Division which was Ingaged. They Sustained a heavy fire for near 20 minutes when they were posted to Cover the Retreat of our

Army & had it not been for this the Retreat must have been attended with great Loss" (quoted in Hammond 1930: 474). Timothy Pickering, an aide to General George Washington, simply noted that "Weedon's brigade, which go up a little before night, fought bravely, and checked the pursuit of the enemy, and gave more time for the others to retreat" (quoted in Pickering 1867: 155).

Despite the intensity of the fire the gathering gloom, which required both sides to engage at close range, also inhibited the effectiveness of the fire. Lieutenant McMichael of the Pennsylvania State Regiment noted that "our regiment fought at one stand about an hour under incessant fire, and yet the loss was less than at Long Island [August 27, 1776]; neither were we so near each other as at Princeton [January 3, 1777], our common distance being about 50 yards" (McMichael 1892: 150). As the 64th Regiment was locked in a desperate firefight, Montresor hurriedly deployed four 12-pdr cannon, which supported an attack by the 33rd Regiment and elements of the 2nd Light Infantry Battalion against Weedon's men deployed in the woods on the flank of the 64th Regiment. As darkness fell the Americans melted into the night and retired toward Chester.

Exhausted from a long day of marching and fighting, the British troops threw themselves down to rest while the Americans retired from the field. Weedon's brigade, forming the rearguard, retired slowly, McMichael recalling that they "marched all night until we neared the town [Chester], when we halted, but not to sleep" (McMichael 1892: 150). Weedon's brigade retired to Chester, Pennsylvania along with the rest of the American army in the aftermath of its defeat at Brandywine. From Chester, Washington moved his army to Germantown, outside of Philadelphia. On September 13, Weedon passed along a laudatory message from the commander in chief to his men: "The General takes the earliest opportunity to return his warmest thanks to the Officers and soldiers of Gen. Weedon's Brigade engaged in the late action for their spirited and soldierly behavior, a conduct so worthy under so many disadvantages cannot fail of establishing to themselves the highest military reputation …" (Weedon 1902: 45–46). Howe and his army remained at Brandywine for four days. During that time detachments were dispatched to secure the surrounding area, collect any remaining American stragglers, and search for American weapons. The 64th Regiment accompanied the army as they occupied the American capital of Philadelphia on September 26.

This grave marker was placed in 1920 to commemorate the soldiers who died during the battle. British returns reported 93 dead and 488 wounded. Although Washington never prepared official returns of American losses during the battle, they are estimated at 300 killed, 600 wounded, and 400 lost as prisoners. The Birmingham Meetinghouse, which prior to the battle had been used by the Americans as a hospital, continued in that role during and after the battle as British surgeons administered to the wounded and the dead were collected in the adjacent graveyard. The dead from both sides were buried along with amputated limbs in a common grave within the walled yard. None of the soldiers buried in the grave was identified. (Author)

Monmouth Courthouse

June 28, 1778

BACKGROUND TO BATTLE

The battle of Monmouth Courthouse in June 1778 would prove to be the first test of the newly trained American Army after the disappointments of the Philadelphia campaign of 1777, which had resulted in the British capture of the Pennsylvanian capital. In February 1778 Frederick William Baron von Steuben joined the American Army in winter quarters at Valley Forge, Pennsylvania, and implemented a training program intended to forge the American Continentals into a fighting force that could stand toe to toe with the British on the field of battle. Throughout the spring Steuben, who was given the rank of major general, oversaw the continuous training of the American regiments. On the morning of June 28, 1778, despite a muddled command structure and a confused advance, the American Continentals at Monmouth would acquit themselves well. In a desperate effort to stall the British advance, secure the retirement of American artillery, and give General Washington time to organize a proper defense, the 2nd Rhode Island Regiment would be deployed at the Parsonage Farm. Opposed to the Rhode Islanders were the veterans of the British 2nd Grenadier Battalion.

In May 1778 Lieutenant-General Sir Henry Clinton replaced Lieutenant-General Howe as British commander-in-chief in Philadelphia. Shortly after arriving, Clinton received several dispatches from Lord George Germain, British Secretary of State for the American Department, directing him to abandon Philadelphia and retire to New York City. The dispatches further ordered Clinton to detach 5,000 men to attack French possessions at St. Lucia, and to send an additional 3,000 men to Florida. To Clinton's further dismay the messages announced that rather than receiving promised reinforcements totaling 12,000 men he should expect only three regiments,

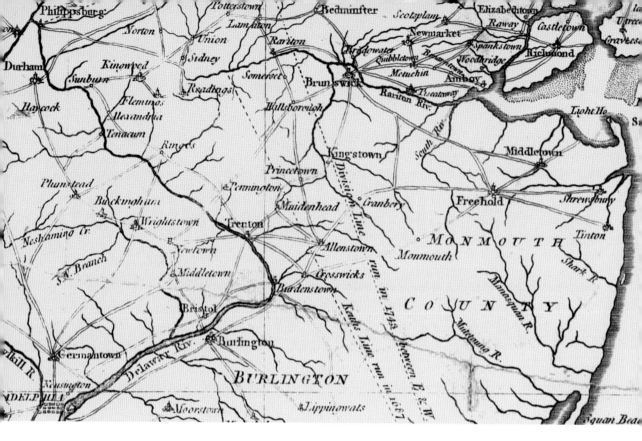

A detail of a map published in June 1780 in London in the *Universal Magazine of Knowledge and Pleasure*, showing the road network of the area around Trenton and Monmouth. Clinton abandoned Philadelphia in June 1778 and marched his men across New Jersey toward New York. Washington's army attacked the British column west of Freehold, New Jersey near Monmouth Courthouse. (Library of Congress)

roughly 1,200 men. Clinton was apprised that future British operations should be directed in the Southern colonies, where there was an expectation that conditions supported British control, while maintaining strong posts at New York and Rhode Island. Although Clinton, after conferring with Howe, briefly considered withdrawing from Philadelphia by sea, on June 18 the British left the city and began an overland march, accompanied by a large group of non-combatants including several thousand Loyalist families.

Having known for several weeks that the British intended to abandon Philadelphia, Washington was immediately informed of the British movement and put his soldiers into motion; he was anxious to test their mettle and engage the British as they marched across New Jersey. Before leaving Valley Forge Washington had convened a council of his generals and asked them whether they thought the American Army should engage Clinton's army. The answer was not encouraging, as only two out of 15 generals supported pursuing a general action. On June 24, as the American Army marched to Hopewell, New Jersey, Washington assembled his generals again and once again was rebuked by a majority. Major General Charles Lee, who had recently rejoined the army after being exchanged from British captivity, argued along with the majority that the Americans should harass the British as they retreated rather than bring on a general action. While disappointing Washington the majority opinion infuriated Brigadier General Wayne, who was joined by Major General Greene in urging Washington to reconsider and bring on a general action with the British.

Washington initially designated a 1,500 man detachment to harass the British rearguard; he offered the command to Lee, who begged off, claiming the size of the force was beneath him. Washington then tapped the Marquis de Lafayette to command the detachment and – in response to news that Clinton had reinforced his rearguard with light infantry and grenadiers – increased the detachment to three divisions, totaling over 5,000 men. The advance guard was made up of a select force, with commanders and men assigned for their battlefield experience. This included units supplemented with "picked men," veterans reassigned from other regiments whose experience allowed them to operate as light infantry. With the expansion of the attack force and at the urging of several officers, Lee reconsidered his previous decision and requested overall command. Washington agreed but assigned Lafayette to command the advance force, composed of a mix of forces under the command of Wayne, Brigadier General Charles Scott, and Brigadier General Maxwell. On the afternoon of June 27 Washington met with his generals and stated his desire that Lee attack the "the rear of the British army as soon as he had information that the front was in motion or marched off" (quoted in Court Martial 1864: 102).

Major General Charles Lee (1731–82) in an engraving from 1775/76. Lee would be largely held responsible for the breakdown of the American attack on the morning of June 28, 1778. Lee, who initially declined the command of the American advance guard, assumed command at the last minute and provided little direction to his subordinates as they began their movement. As his forces engaged the British rearguard, Lee remained aloof despite repeated requests for additional orders. Lacking firm direction and under increasing pressure from the British, Lee's command collapsed. Although he conducted a credible retreat, Lee's conduct was widely criticized and in response Lee criticized General George Washington. He was brought up on charges and court-martialed in July 1778. Lee was convicted of disobedience and disrespect for the commander-in-chief, and relieved of command for one year. He subsequently retired from the Army in disgrace. (ASKB)

The 2nd Rhode Island Regiment traced its origin back to the organization of Colonel Daniel Hitchcock's Regiment in May 1775 as part of the Rhode Island Army of Observation. In early 1776 the regiment was redesignated as the 11th Continental Regiment; it fought with Washington's army throughout the campaign around New York and retreated across New Jersey in December 1776. At that time the unit was again redesignated the 2nd Rhode Island Regiment and accompanied the American army at 2nd Trenton and Princeton in January 1777. After a brief deployment to defend the Hudson Valley, the 2nd Rhode Island rejoined the main army in time to resist the British advance towards Philadelphia in 1777. In October 1777, along with the 1st Rhode Island, the regiment won a victory at Red Bank and elements of the unit helped defend Fort Mifflin. The regiment endured the desperate winter at Valley Forge, training with Steuben. In early 1778 the officers of the 1st Rhode Island were detached to return home to recruit a new regiment, while the enlisted men were transferred to the 2nd Rhode Island.

Brigadier General James Varnum's brigade, numbering only 300 men, was commanded by Colonel John Durkee, and composed of the combined 1st and 2nd Rhode Island regiments under Lieutenant Colonel Jeremiah Olney, the 4th and 8th Connecticut regiments under Durkee's command, and a two-gun 3-pdr artillery section commanded by Captain David Cook. Joseph Plumb Martin, serving as a private in the 8th Connecticut, noted that "the officer who commanded the platoon that I belonged to was a captain, belonging to the Rhode Island troops …" (quoted in Martin 1993: 126), suggesting there was an excess of officers in the composite Rhode Island regiment. Despite absorbing men from the 1st Rhode Island the 2nd Rhode Island totaled no more than 150 men. The combined 4th and 8th Connecticut regiments were somewhat smaller in size.

MAP KEY

1 1130hrs: Major General Charles Lee's American forces fall back in the face of an aggressive British pursuit.

2 1135hrs: Captain Seward and Captain Cook's two-gun sections deploy to fire on the advancing British columns.

3 1140hrs: The British Grenadiers, Guards, Light Dragoons, and artillery pursue the Americans.

4 1145hrs: Ordered into the Point of Woods, the 2nd Pennsylvania (Colonel Walter Stewart) and 3rd Maryland (Lieutenant Colonel Nathaniel Ramsay) briefly exchange fire with the 1st Guards Battalion and elements of the 1st Grenadier Battalion. Cook and Seward's artillery retires.

5 1150hrs: Stewart and Ramsey's men retire; as they emerge from the woods they are attacked by Light Dragoons.

6 1150hrs: Lee deploys the 4th New York, 2nd Rhode Island, and 4th/8th Connecticut regiments along the hedge-fence. Cook's artillery deploys while Seward's retires.

7 1155hrs: Wayne deploys Stewart's and Ramsay's men in the woods north of the Englishtown Road.

8 1200hrs: The 16th Light Dragoons and 2nd Grenadier Battalion resume their advance. The 1st Grenadier Battalion and Guards Brigade advance along the Englishtown Road.

9 1210hrs: The 1st Grenadier Battalion attacks the 2nd Pennsylvania and 3rd Maryland, forcing them to retire.

10 1215hrs: A squadron of the 16th Light Dragoons advances towards the hedge-fence and is driven off by musket fire. The British cavalry moves south to cross the hedge-fence and outflank the American position.

11 1220hrs: The 2nd Grenadier Battalion advances in a disorganized column and is met with intense artillery and musket fire; its commander, Colonel Henry Monckton, is killed.

12 1225hrs: Seeing the 16th Light Dragoons moving around the American right flank, Lieutenant Colonel Eleazer Oswald orders Cook's artillery to retire.

13 1230hrs: Major General William Alexander (Lord Stirling)'s force, including ten guns, deploys along the ridge.

14 1230hrs: The British 3rd Brigade advances in pursuit of the scattered elements of Brigadier General Charles Scott's command near the Craig Farm.

15 1235hrs: As the 2nd Grenadier Battalion resumes its assault, Lee recognizes the threat of envelopment; he orders the 4th New York, 2nd Rhode Island, and 4th/8th Connecticut to retire and retreat over the causeway.

16 1240hrs: The 2nd Grenadier Battalion pursues the Americans until halted by artillery fire from Perrine Ridge. The grenadiers retire into the wooded areas along the creek.

17 1250hrs: Deploying near the Parsonage Farm, the British artillery initiates a prolonged duel with the American artillery on Perrine Ridge.

18 1255hrs: The 2nd Battalion, 42nd (Royal Highland) Regiment advances toward Perrine Ridge; taken under artillery fire, it takes cover in an adjacent orchard. The remainder of the 3rd Brigade deploys east of the Sutfin Farm.

19 1450hrs: Greene marches to Combs Hill, which outflanks the Parsonage Farm position, and deploys four 6-pdr guns.

20 1500hrs: Colonel Joseph Cilley and Colonel Richard Parker's composite battalions advance against the 2/42nd Regiment. After an initial exchange of musket fire, the Highlanders slowly fall back, followed by the Americans.

21 1515hrs: Clinton orders a general retirement.

22 1530hrs: Wayne orders three regiments across the causeway to attack the British rearguard.

23 1545hrs: Wayne's command attacks the 1st Grenadier Battalion, which is reinforced by the 33rd Regiment.

24 1600hrs: The British drive the Americans back. American artillery on Comb's Hill forces the British to retire to rejoin Clinton's main column at Monmouth Courthouse.

Battlefield environment

Between Monmouth Courthouse in the east and Perrine Ridge to the west, the ground is characterized by rolling farmland, bordered by fences and interspersed by watercourses and woodlots. The nature of the Monmouth terrain channeled movement along narrow corridors rather than allowing for coordinated movement across a wide front. The Englishtown Road, along which the Americans would advance, ran east to west and intersected the Allentown Road at Monmouth Courthouse. The East Ravine which the Americans crossed to attack the British rearguard was northeast of the Englishtown Road and formed by the Spotswood Middle Brook. From the East Morass the Middle Brook meandered west, parallel to the Englishtown Road. The Englishtown Road crossed through the Point of Woods and crossed the Middle Ravine formed by a tributary of the Middle Brook. West of the Point of Woods and south of the Englishtown Road were the Wikoff, Rhea, and Parsonage farms. West of the Parsonage Farm the Englishtown Road crossed the Middle Brook in an area known as the West Ravine, along a timbered causeway before angling northwest through the Sutfin Farm and rising to the Perrine Ridge.

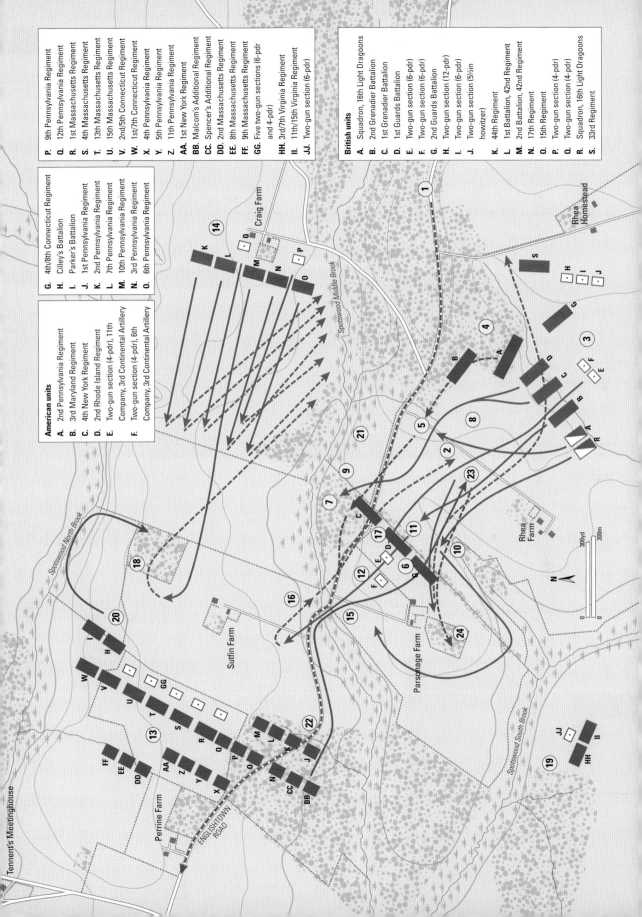

American units

A. 2nd Maryland Regiment
B. 3rd Maryland Regiment
C. 4th New York Regiment
D. 2nd Rhode Island Regiment
E. Two-gun section (4-pdr), 11th Company, 3rd Continental Artillery
F. Two-gun section (4-pdr), 6th Company, 3rd Continental Artillery
G. 4th/8th Connecticut Regiment
H. Cilley's Battalion
I. Parker's Battalion
J. 1st Pennsylvania Regiment
K. 2nd Pennsylvania Regiment
L. 7th Pennsylvania Regiment
M. 10th Pennsylvania Regiment
N. 3rd Pennsylvania Regiment
O. 6th Pennsylvania Regiment
P. 9th Pennsylvania Regiment
Q. 12th Pennsylvania Regiment
R. 1st Massachusetts Regiment
S. 4th Massachusetts Regiment
T. 13th Massachusetts Regiment
U. 15th Massachusetts Regiment
V. 2nd/5th Massachusetts Regiment
W. 1st/7th Connecticut Regiment
X. 4th Pennsylvania Regiment
Y. 5th Pennsylvania Regiment
Z. 11th Pennsylvania Regiment
AA. 1st New York Regiment
BB. Malcom's Additional Regiment
CC. Spencer's Additional Regiment
DD. 2nd Massachusetts Regiment
EE. 8th Massachusetts Regiment
FF. 9th Massachusetts Regiment
GG. Five two-gun sections (6-pdr and 4-pdr)
HH. 3rd/7th Virginia Regiment
II. 11th/15th Virginia Regiment
JJ. Two-gun section (6-pdr)

British units

A. Squadron, 16th Light Dragoons
B. 2nd Grenadier Battalion
C. 1st Grenadier Battalion
D. 1st Guards Battalion
E. Two-gun section (6-pdr)
F. Two-gun section (6-pdr)
G. 2nd Guards Battalion
H. Two-gun section (12-pdr)
I. Two-gun section (6-pdr)
J. Two-gun section (5½in howitzer)
K. 44th Regiment
L. 1st Battalion, 42nd Regiment
M. 2nd Battalion, 42nd Regiment
N. 17th Regiment
O. 15th Regiment
P. Two-gun section (4-pdr)
Q. Two-gun section (4-pdr)
R. Squadron, 16th Light Dragoons
S. 33rd Regiment

INTO COMBAT

Elements of Lee's command reported receiving orders to prepare to march between 0200hrs and 0300hrs on June 28 and the majority were in motion by 0400hrs. Colonel William Grayson marched his advance guard, composed of Varnum's brigade, under the command of Colonel John Durkee, and a detachment from Scott's brigade, to Englishtown. Most of the men were unable to prepare a meal before being ordered to draw their provisions and an allotment of rum; Joseph Plumb Martin wrote that "we were early in the morning mustered out and ordered to leave all our baggage under the care of a guard, taking only our blankets and provisions …" (quoted in Martin 1993: 76).

Having spent the night of June 27/28 encamped around St. Peter's Church, scattered houses and a wooden courthouse, the British intended to march northeast towards Middletown and then Sandy Hook. At 0400hrs Knyphausen's 2nd Division, forming the British vanguard, commenced its march, followed by a 12-mile-long line of wagons. The British rearguard, which Lee intended to attack, had already begun its withdrawal as the Americans approached the Tennent Friends Meetinghouse on their way to Monmouth Courthouse. With news that the British were continuing their march east, Washington put the American army in motion. While a series of deep ravines and morasses that cut across the main Englishtown Road slowed movement, they did provide some relief from the heat of the day. "We had to fall back again as soon as we could into the woods; by the time we got under the shade of the trees and had taken a breath, of which we had been almost deprived …"(quoted in Martin 1993: 76).

Lacking credible intelligence and receiving contradictory information about the size and composition of the British opposition, Lee ordered Durkee to cross and then re-cross the West Morass several times. Lee himself testified that he was "mortified and chagrined, particularly as it occasioned distress to Colonel Durgee's [Durkee] corps, by little marches and counter-marches from one hill to another over the ravine …" (quoted in Court Martial 1864: 204). Despite these impediments, Lee was encouraged when he received word that the British rearguard numbered only 2,000 men, directing Lafayette to assume command over Scott's and Wayne's men and attempt to cut off the British force.

Although initially surprised by the American attack in strength, Clinton and Lieutenant-General Lord Cornwallis quickly issued orders recalling additional forces, which included the 1st and 2nd Grenadier battalions and the Guards Brigade, to support the rearguard. The 2nd Grenadier Battalion was composed of the grenadier companies of the 37th, 40th, 43rd, 44th, 45th, 46th, 49th, 52nd, 54th, 57th, 63rd, and 64th regiments. Captain John Peebles of the 42nd (Royal Highland) Regiment's Grenadier Company, serving in the 1st Grenadier Battalion, noted that "Between 9 & 10 o'clock when our Brigade was about 4 miles advanced from the Village of Monmouth, (the Rear of the Division I suppose about 2 miles behind) the Enemy made their appearance in force near the Rear; the General rode back & ordered the troops to face about and march back with all speed to attack the Rebels …" (quoted in Gruber 1997: 193).

The American advance became confused as it pushed forward but in several fits and starts Lee's men engaged the

The Monmouth battlefield was largely defined by the various branches of the Spotsburg Brook. The Middle Brook wound its way through the center of the battlefield and along its banks soggy ground and vegetation restricted movement. Along the Brook the ground was covered with thick vegetation, giving cover to the American defenders and significantly restricting movement by both sides. Adding to the difficulty of crossing the Middle Brook itself there were numerous smaller tributaries feeding in to the main waterway. These areas, described as a morass, allowed American troops to delay the British advance. The British grenadiers found the heat unbearable, Lieutenant William Hale of the 2nd Grenadier Battalion hoping that "… such a march I may never again experience. We proceeded five miles on a road composed of nothing but sand which scorched through our shoes with intolerable heat; the sun beating on our heads with a force scarcely to be conceived in Europe, and not a drop of water to assuage our parching thirst" (quoted in Wilkin 1914: 258). (Author)

British rearguard near the Monmouth Courthouse between 0930hrs and 1000hrs. By 1000hrs Wayne, Scott, and Maxwell's men began to form and Lieutenant Colonel Oswald brought several cannon across the East Ravine and exchanged shots with the British artillery. Finding his battery unsupported, Oswald appealed to Lieutenant Colonel John Laurens, one of Washington's aides-de-camp, to request assistance from Major General Lee. Lee initially detached Olney's 2nd Rhode Island with orders to attack a body of troops thought to be British, but after they turned out to be Americans, Olney deployed his men. He later recalled:

> I marched the regiment out on the plain and formed the line in view of the enemy, where I halted a few minutes; but seeing the enemy was advancing in column from their left and our troops retiring, I then wheeled the regiment by platoons to the right and marched off to the brigade but before I had joined them I was met by General Lee and General Wayne, who ordered me to move on and to cover the artillery under Colonel Oswald. (Quoted in Court Martial 1864:145–46)

After marching a short distance Olney found that Oswald's artillery had already retreated. During the ensuing exchange of cannon fire Durkee was severely wounded along with several officers of the 2nd Rhode Island. With Durkee's wounding, Olney took over command of Varnum's brigade.

Clinton noted that the American right flank was vulnerable and began to shift his reinforcements in that direction. As Lee shuffled individual units into provisional task forces the overall command-and-control structure began to unravel. After a short exchange with the British artillery Oswald requested permission to retire. As he did so, covered by Varnum's brigade, Scott and Maxwell also became concerned about their exposed positions and the deteriorating tactical situation; having no further directions from Lee, they retired, with Lafayette following suit. By 1115hrs Lee's entire command was streaming back towards the west.

Although Clinton was somewhat reluctant to pursue the retreating Americans after blunting the initial attack on his rearguard, the rapidity and confusion of the American retirement seemed to offer an opportunity for a decisive engagement. Clinton deployed the British 1st and 2nd Grenadier battalions and the Guards Brigade from left to right, supported by elements of the 16th Light Dragoons, Queen's Rangers, and British light infantry. Lieutenant Colonel Elisha Lawrence of the 2nd New Jersey testified that the British "were then advancing in two columns, with their artillery and cavalry between the columns" (quoted in Court Martial 1864: 62) while Hale simply noted: "the Grenadiers were ordered to the right about and march to the heights of which the Rebels were already possessed …" (quoted in Wilkin 1914: 257). Seeing the British advancing rapidly, Lee ordered Colonel Walter Stewart, 13th Pennsylvania, and Lieutenant Colonel Nathaniel Ramsey, 3rd Maryland, to deploy their regiments to cover the retreat; he also directed Colonel Henry Livingston's 4th New York to protect Oswald's battery. After a long morning of march and countermarch across ravines and fences and through wooded lots under a blazing summer sun, the men of Lee's command were exhausted. Despite this, Oswald continued to use his artillery to slow the advance of the main British force.

A British grenadier of the 6th Regiment of Foot; a 1778 pencil and ink drawing by Philip James de Loutherberg (1740–1812). At this time the 6th Regiment was back in Britain, having served briefly in America in the latter part of 1776. This grenadier is adopting position 2, "Cock your firelock," in *The Manual Exercise* of 1764; his smart, parade-ground bearing contrasts dramatically with the likely appearance of the British grenadiers at Monmouth Courthouse. Since leaving Philadelphia on June 17 the British army had endured temperatures above 90 degrees coupled with high humidity and drenching thunderstorms in the late afternoon and evenings. Although the Americans also suffered through the summer heat, they were able to shed their heavy wool uniforms and carried a minimum of supplies. On June 28 British and American participants commented on the excessive heat of the day, some estimating the temperature rose above 100 degrees during the afternoon. (ASKB)

Washington at Monmouth, an engraving by George R. Hall published in 1858. After hearing reports that Major General Lee's advance guard was in full retreat, at about 1100hrs Washington rode forward to the Tennent Friends Meetinghouse, where he heard from a young fifer that the Americans were retreating from Monmouth Courthouse. Washington continued forward to confront his subordinate, demanding to know why Lee was retreating. Lee's response, claiming both a lack of intelligence and that his orders were not being obeyed, did not placate Washington, who remarked that Lee should not have requested to command if he did not intend to attack. Washington directed Wayne to take deploy Stewart's 13th Pennsylvania and Ramsey's 3rd Maryland on the left of the road, before asking Lee if he would command the rearguard while Washington organized a defense along Perrine Farm ridge, which commanded the ground beyond the ravine. (Library of Congress)

At about 1140hrs Washington confronted Lee and took direct command of the American defense. The ground selected by Washington to form a defensive line was along the Englishtown Road, just west of the Middle Ravine, at the boundary between the Parsonage and Rhea farms. The boundary line between the two farms was formed by a split-rail fence along which vegetation, including small trees and shrubs, had grown, forming a hedge-like appearance. The defense of the hedge-fence was borne by Livingston's 4th New York and the Rhode Island and Connecticut regiments of Varnum's brigade. Although Lee was responsible for the overall defense of the Parsonage Farm, several other prominent officers were present and assisted in preparing to meet the British assault. Lieutenant Colonel Alexander Hamilton, Washington's aide, related: "I found Colonel Olney retreating with a part of General Varnum's brigade; I pressed him to form his troops along a fence which was near him, which he immediately performed and had a sharp conflict with the enemy" (quoted in Court Martial 1864: 69). Olney recalled that "Colonel Hamilton rode up to the brigade and ordered us to form with all possible dispatch, or he feared the artillery in front would be lost, and by the time we had formed the enemy had advanced within good musket shot …" (Court Martial 1864: 146–47). While the bulk of the American artillery retreated over the Spotswood Middle Brook towards the Perrine Farm ridge, Oswald "brought up the rear with Captain Cook's two pieces and placed them on an eminence just in the rear of the hedge-row" (Court Martial 1864: 158), where they were supported by Livingston's 4th New York and other units of Varnum's brigade.

As Lee organized the defense of the crossing over the Spotswood Middle Brook causeway the British continued to advance, pushing the disorganized Americans before them. At length the British approached the American line at the Parsonage Farm. The British were deployed with elements of the 16th Light Dragoons on their left flank. The 2nd Grenadier Battalion deployed south of the Englishtown Road, moving directly towards Livingston's and Olney's men situated along the hedge-fence. The 1st Grenadier Battalion, supported by elements of the Guards Brigade, opposed the 13th Pennsylvania and the 3rd Maryland in the woods north of the Englishtown Road. Lieutenant Hale described the advance: "… marching through a cornfield we saw them drawn up behind a morass on a hill with a rail fence in front and a thick wood on their left filled with their light chosen troops … [Approaching the Parsonage Farm] we rose on a small hill commanded by that on which they were posted in excellent order notwithstanding a heavy fire of Grape" (quoted in Wilkin 1914: 257–59). Captain Peebles wrote:

> … about 2 miles to the westwd of the Village the Gr[enadie]rs attack'd & the Light Infy. were sent to the right. The 1st Battn. Light Infantry & Queens Rangers were dispatch'd to the right to try to gain the Enemy's left flank, but meeting swamps and much impediments in the Woods they did not get up in time, mean while the Brigade of Guards & two Battalions of British Grenrs. after a very quick march moved up briskly & attack'd the Enemy … (Quoted in Gruber 1997: 193)

In their enthusiasm to come to grips with the enemy, having overwhelmed every attempt by the Americans to stall their advance, the British attack took on a frenzied character and as a result became more disorganized. Everywhere the Americans had attempted to stand and delay the British advance the defenders had been forced to retreat in disorder. As the British grenadiers and Foot Guards surged forward towards the Spotswood Middle Brook, American resistance began to stiffen. The 16th Light Dragoons, moving quickly up the rising ground on the British left flank, charged the Americans waiting behind the hedge-fence. Sergeant Jeremiah Greenman of the 2nd Rhode Island wrote "we form'd again under a fence ware [*sic*] the light horse advanced on us. We began a fire on them very heavy …" (Greenman 1978: 122). Laurens observed that: "Two regiments were formed behind a [hedge] fence in front of the position. The enemy's horse advanced in full charge with admirable bravery to the distance of forty paces, when a general discharge from these regiments did great execution among them, and made them fly with the greatest precipitation" (quoted in Lee Papers 1873: 197). Unable to penetrate the strong American position along the hedge-fence, the British cavalry retired, leaving the Americans to reload as the grenadiers surged towards them.

The area of British approach was constrained north of the Englishtown Road by the Spotswood Middle Brook. The area south of the road, made up of fields of the Rhea Farm, extended to the Spotswood South Brook. Moving quickly in column, the British grenadiers appear to have been ordered to assault the American line without deploying. As the American organized their defensive line at the hedge-fence at the Parsonage Farm, the British, having driven the Americans over almost 2 miles of broken ground from the Monmouth Courthouse, were more of a disorganized mob than a disciplined fighting force. Hale later wrote: "when judge of my inexpressible surprise, General Clinton himself appeared at the head of our left wing, accompanied by Lord Cornwallis, and crying out 'Charge, Grenadiers, never heed forming' …" (quoted in Wilkin 1914: 259). Hale goes on to describe the haphazard assault, contending, "it was no longer a contest for bringing up our reserve companies in the best order, but all officers as well as soldiers strove who could be foremost, to my shame I speak it" (quoted in Wilkin 1914: 259).

The contest at the hedgerow did not last long but the intensity of the combat was commented on by several participants. Peebles described the approach against the American position at the hedge-fence: "After a very quick march moved up briskly & attack'd the Enemy in front receiving a heavy fire as they approach'd of both cannon and musketry & when within a short distance they pour'd in their fire …" (quoted in Gruber 1997: 193–94). Hale also confirmed the intensity of combat: "… we rushed on amidst the heaviest fire I have yet felt" (quoted in Wilkin 1914: 259). Captain John Cumpston, an artillery officer serving with Cook's section on the small hill to the rear of the hedge-fence, recalled that the battery

formed in the rear of a party of troops that were to cover our pieces. The enemy were then advancing; a very heavy fire began of musquetry in our front and left wing. General Knox

The approach of the 2nd Grenadier Battalion to the hedge-fence was up a slightly rising slope, shielding the American position from view until the defenders were within close range. The fenceline was broken up with stands of vegetation. As the British advanced in the sweltering midday heat Lieutenant Hale was hard pressed to keep his men in good order. Although he directed his sergeants to close ranks, the men of the 45th Grenadier Company followed the lead of their neighboring companies and quickened their step as they advanced up the slope towards the hedge-fence. The fence, overgrown in places, hid the strength of the American defenders. (Author)

Jeremiah Greenman was born in Newport, Rhode Island on May 7, 1758 and enlisted in the Continental Army during the summer of 1775. Serving as a private on Benedict Arnold's expedition to Quebec in September that year, he was captured during the assault on Quebec and held prisoner until he was paroled in August 1776. He reenlisted in the Rhode Island Continentals in February 1777 as a sergeant and by the end of 1777 was promoted to first sergeant of the 2nd Rhode Island Regiment. During 1777 Greenman fought at Red Bank and Fort Mifflin. Wounded at Monmouth and then promoted to ensign in 1779, Greenman would be wounded again at the battle of Springfield on June 23, 1780. Greenman was promoted to 1st lieutenant in May 1781, the same day he was captured by Loyalist troops. Paroled in October 1781, he became the regimental adjutant in 1782. In 1783 he was mustered out of the Continental Army; he returned to Providence, Rhode Island and became a shopkeeper, dying on November 15, 1828, aged 70.

gave us ... orders to give the enemy a shot. I believe our people made a stand there about two minutes; after giving them two or three charges of grape shot, we were ordered to retire ... across the morass. (Quoted in Court Martial 1864: 142)

Oswald recalled that "Through the breaches that had been made in the fence I discharged several grapes of shot at the enemy, the infantry being engaged with them" (quoted in Court Martial 1864: 156). Officers on both sides were conspicuous as they rallied their men. Lieutenant Colonel Hamilton later testified that "It was only after this that I assisted in forming the troops under Colonel Olney. In the action they had with the enemy my horse received a wound, which occasioned me a fall, by which I was considerably hurt. This and previous fatigue obliged me to retire ..." (quoted in Court Martial 1864: 70–71). Laurens was also wounded as he rallied the men defending the hedge-fence: "The grenadiers succeeded to the attack. At this time my horse was killed under me. In this spot the action was hottest and there was considerable slaughter of the British grenadiers" (Laurens 1867: 197).

Lieutenant Hale rallied his men after the initial American volley crashed into the tightly packed grenadier ranks. Around him the dead and wounded hampered his efforts to help his sergeants restore order and resume the attack. Many of his men had stopped and begun to fire their muskets through the haze created by the American volleys. Hale and his sergeants ordered the men to stop firing and charge forward using their bayonets. Slowly the British grenadiers closed the distance to the hedge-fence. Although the Americans' initial volleys staggered the British grenadiers, the weight of the British attack quickly began to threaten the American position. Olney described the deteriorating American position:

> ... the two pieces of artillery had got nearly to the fence, and as soon as they had passed into our rear we began to fire, and after exchanging about ten rounds with them we were obliged to retreat with considerable loss on each side, but not till after the enemy outflanked us and had advanced quite up to the fence by which we were formed. (Quoted in Court Martial 1864: 146–47)

In addition to the continued pressure from the grenadiers, the horsemen of the 16th Light Dragoons began to work their way around the American right flank, which was anchored along the hedge-fence. Joseph Plumb Martin noted:

OPPOSITE
Published in Augsburg in 1776, these engravings by Johann Martin Will (1727–1806) depict an American soldier. The figures are shown wearing the linen hunting shirt and overalls that popularized the image of the American soldiers throughout the Revolutionary War. First used by riflemen, hunting shirts were more comfortable and allowed greater freedom of movement than the traditional uniform. The shirts could be made of from homespun linen or buckskin and were sometimes adorned with fringes. While most shirts were undyed, over the course of the war shirts appeared in a wide range of colors, including green, purple, and blue. General Washington recommended that the hunting shirt be adopted as the primary American uniform. Throughout the war hunting shirts were issued to units as standard uniforms, in many cases due to ease of availability and lower cost. In early 1778 the 2nd Rhode Island Regiment was issued hunting shirts and wore the shirts at Monmouth. (ASKB)

William Hale

William John Hale, son of a British admiral, was born in Charleston, South Carolina in 1756. Commissioned a lieutenant in the 45th Regiment in March 1776 and assigned to the Grenadier Company, Hale participated in Howe's offensive around New York that June. Hale was later detached from his company and joined a column of recruits; in early January 1777 his column was attacked near Princeton by the main American army. Although Hale escaped capture, he suffered a minor wound. Hale fought at Brandywine; although not engaged at Germantown (October 4, 1777), the 2nd Grenadier Battalion pursued the retreating American army. Hale's unit then garrisoned Philadelphia before fighting at Monmouth Courthouse. Casualties among the 2nd Grenadier Battalion were heavy, although Hale escaped unhurt. When the 2nd Grenadier Battalion was broken up, Hale's company rejoined the 45th Regiment; in 1779 the depleted unit, numbering around 100 including Hale, returned to Britain. In March 1780 Hale was promoted captain in the 94th Regiment. Retiring in December 1781, he married in 1783 and retired to Chudleigh, Devonshire where he died in 1789 aged only 33.

By the time the British had come in contact with the New England forces at the fence, when a sharp conflict ensued. These troops maintained their ground, till the whole force of the enemy that could be brought to bear had charged upon them through the fence; and after being overpowered by numbers and the platoon officers had given orders for their several platoons to leave the fence, they had to force them to retreat, so eager were they to be revenged on the invaders of their country and rights. (Quoted in Martin 1993: 78)

Olney described the ferocity of the British attack: "We formed in a line in front of a morass, and began a fire with musketry. The enemy came on with such impetuosity that they turned our right flank, which threw us into disorder, and we retreated" (quoted in Williams 1839: 245). Greenman noticed that the Connecticut troops on his right had begun to retire from the hedge-fence as the order to retreat was passed along the line. On the American left the 1st Grenadier Battalion pushed the two American regiments out of the woods. Captain Mercer recounted:

Americaner Soldat.

I there saw the Commanding Officer, who I did not know, and who told him that General Lee's orders were, that he should defend that wood to the last extremity, and cover the retreat of the whole at the bridge: he replied, that the enemy had got upon his left, and they were very good men, and it would never do to have them sacrificed there. When I returned to General Lee, the [British] light-horse had charged upon the right of the troops in the woods, and were mixed amongst them as they retreated out of the wood seemingly mixed with our troops, and the action between Colonel Livingston's regiment and General Varnum's brigade with the enemy then commenced; they were soon broke by a charge of the enemy. (Quoted in Court Martial 1864: 130)

As the British cavalry moved to threaten the American flank and the infantry began to drift away from the hedge-fence, Oswald ordered the American artillery to retreat. Knox also related that he

Americaner Soldat.

desired Lieutenant Colonel Olney to take post at a hedge fence in front of a bridge over which we retreated. At this time, the enemy's light horse were making a rapid movement upon our right, and we had retired with the pieces in the rear of the

The American stand at the Parsonage Farm

British view: As the American forces retired in disorder, closely pursued by the 1st and 2nd Grenadier battalions, the 2nd Rhode Island was ordered to defend a fence line overgrown with vegetation at the Parsonage Farm. The British grenadiers, dressed in their bearskins and suffering from the suffocating midday heat and humidity, found themselves moving slightly uphill towards the American line, which erupted in a sheet of fire. The grenadiers, disorganized after their pursuit and staggered by the American volley stopped to return fire. The first line of grenadiers are shown here loading and firing while the men behind move up in support and file off to the right to extend the line and bring more muskets to bear on the Americans. Lieutenant-Colonel Henry Monckton, commanding the 2nd Grenadier Battalion, was killed attempting to dislodge the Rhode Island Continentals.

American view: In a desperate attempt to stem the relentless British advance and allow retreating artillery to cross a narrow causeway over the Middlebrook morass, Continentals from the 2nd Rhode Island Regiment were deployed along the split-rail fence. Supported by two 3-pdr guns, the Rhode Island Continentals, dressed predominantly in hunting shirts or shirtsleeves, fired on the advancing British grenadiers. After the first volleys the firing has become more disorganized with individual soldiers reloading and firing at will at the mass of British grenadiers re-forming 50yd away. While the hedge-fence provides some cover for the Rhode Islanders, the smoke from musket-fire has combined with the haze of the midday heat to obscure the enemy.

front, and from a wood on the left, and the movements of the enemy horse on our right obliged us to retire over the bridge … (Quoted in Court Martial 1864: 181)

Although the American infantry now began to retire they had blunted the British advance, gaining enough time to allow the two cannon to limber and fall back. Oswald thought the lack of British coordination saved the American battery: "… had the enemy charged with spirit, I think I must inevitably have lost some pieces upon the last hill, when the enemy's horse had charged upon the right … the enemy being retiring, had the enemy pushed on with spirit they must have taken the two pieces" (quoted in Court Martial 1864: 158). After the brief defense of the hedge-fence, Oswald's artillery limbered and moved across the Middle Brook morass, followed by Olney's infantry. As he had promised Washington, Major General Lee was among the last to cross the causeway: "These battalions having sustained with gallantry and returned with vigor a very considerable fire, were at length successively forced over the bridge; the rear I brought up myself" (quoted in Court Martial 1864: 217). The British pursued the retreating Americans across the causeway. Captain Peebles described the grenadiers

> dashing forward drove the enemy before them for a considerable time, killing many with their Bayonets but seeing a fresh line of the Enemy strongly posted on t'other side [of] a Ravine & Swamp & well supplied with Cannon & having suffer'd much both from the fire of the Enemy and & fatigue & heat of the day, they were order'd to retire … (Quoted in Gruber 1997: 193–94)

As they pushed forward the British were brought under fire by the American artillery deployed on Perrine Ridge. The British quickly brought up their guns and for the next several hours both sides engaged in a prolonged artillery duel. Lieutenant Hale along with the men of the 2nd Grenadier Battalion pushed forward: "With some difficulty we were brought under the hill we had gained, and the most terrible cannonade [Brigadier-General] L[or]d W. Erskine [Clinton's quartermaster general] says he ever heard ensued and lasted for two hours, at the distance of 600 yards" (quoted in Wilkin 1914: 259). The British grenadiers found themselves unable to advance, due to the strong American position on Perrine Ridge, and unable to retire. Hale described the grenadiers' situation: "The shattered remains of our Battalion being under cover of our hill suffered little, but from thirst and heat of which several died, except some who preferred the shade of some trees in the direct range of shot … Capt. Powell of the 52nd Grenadiers, one of these had his arm shattered to pieces …" (quoted in Wilkin 1914: 259).

While the British advance was stalled by the strong American deployment along Perrine Ridge, Major General Greene moved his division onto Combs Hill on the British left flank. The American position was well protected by the Middle Brook morass and allowed American artillery to enfilade the British line. Unable to turn the American right flank, Clinton dispatched the 42nd

A view along the hedge-fence looking south. South of the deployed 3-pdr artillery, the 2nd Rhode Island Regiment occupied the hedge-fence in this general area; farther to the south, elements of the 4th and 8th Connecticut regiments were deployed. The American defenders at the hedge-fence were largely combat-tested veterans who had survived the desperate winter at Valley Forge and endured Steuben's rigorous training program. Despite having marched and fought throughout the morning in excessive heat the men of the 2nd Rhode Island, 8th Connecticut, and 4th New York remained steady. The Americans waited until the grenadiers had closed to effective range before opening fire. Hale noted that "the Rebels' Cannon playing Grape and Case upon us at the distance of 40 yards and the small arms within little more than half that space" (quoted in Wilkin 1914: 262–63), while Greenman later recorded simply that "then the footmen rushed on us. After firing a Number of rounds we was obliged to retreat" (Greenman 1978: 122). During the course of the battle at the hedge-fence Greenman was wounded in the thigh. (Author)

Brigadier General Anthony Wayne is depicted in this work by Albert Rosenthal, published in 1902. Wayne served under Lee during the attack on the British rearguard and helped organize American troops during the retreat. Wayne retired to Perrine Ridge and as the British began their retreat, commanded a group of Pennsylvania regiments that fought an inconclusive action against the British rearguard. (Library of Congress)

(Royal Highland) Regiment (3rd Brigade) to probe the American left flank. The Americans responded by dispatching several regiments to challenge the British advance, also taking the enemy under artillery fire from the Perrine Ridge. Outnumbered and outflanked, the British retired. As the cannonade fell away later that afternoon, Clinton ordered a general retirement. Seeing the British disengaging, Washington directed Wayne to advance with the 3rd Pennsylvania, Malcolm's, and Spencer's Additional regiments to harass the enemy. The British grenadiers again formed the British rearguard as they retired. Having stymied the American pursuit, the British rearguard retired to Monmouth Courthouse.

As the sun set on both armies, they took stock of their losses. The British lamented the death of Colonel Monckton, the commander of the 2nd Grenadier Battalion, killed during the assault on the hedge-fence; Hale later wrote: "Colonel Monckton was shot through the heart at the first charge, to the unspeakable loss of the Regt ... his body which could not be found in the spot where he fell by a party I sent to bury it, was intered by the Rebels the next day ..." (quoted in Wilkin 1914: 259). Hale also noted other casualties: "Lt. Kennedy of the 44th Grenadiers ... was killed by the same fire ... Our battalion lost 98, 11 officers killed and wounded, Major Gardner [10th Regiment] shot very badly through the foot" (Wilkin 1914: 259–60). He went on to write in July 1778, "Major Gardner is yet in a doubtful situation, the ball cannot be extracted, and the loss of the leg is extremely feared. Colonel Trelawney [1st Guards Battalion] who was left with Rebels is here in a fair way of recovery ..." (quoted in Wilkin 1914: 264). Captain Peebles also chronicled losses among the grenadier battalions: "In this action the Grenrs. suffer'd considerably having 13 officers killed and wounded and about 150 men killed wounded & missing Colo: Monckton among the slain. The Guards likewise lost above 40 ..." (quoted in Gruber 1997: 194).

While Washington expected the British to renew the struggle in the morning, Peebles described Clinton's decision to retire:

> ... it was thought improper to advance any further upon the enemy of Monmouth where the wounded and Sick were brought to in the Evening – where we remained till near 12 oclock at night & leaving those of the wounded that were too ill remove, with a Surgeon & flag we march'd forward to join the other division of the Army whom we overtook near Middletown at 9 o'clock of the morning of the 29th. (Quoted in Gruber 1997: 194)

While Lee's advance failed to cut off the British rearguard and the resulting battle exposed continuing problems with the command-and-control structure of Washington's army, the performance of individual units during the course of the action proved the value of Steuben's rigorous training. Lieutenant Colonel Hamilton, a harsh critic of the performance of American soldiers, wrote approvingly:

> The behavior of the officers and men in general was such as could not easily be surpassed. Our troops, after the first impulse from mismanagement, behaved with more spirit& moved with greater order than the British troops. You know my way of thinking about our army, and that I am not apt to flatter it. I assure you I never was pleased with them before this day. (Quoted in Syrett & Cooke 1961: 513)

Cowpens

January 17, 1781

BACKGROUND TO BATTLE

The clash between American troops under Major General Daniel Morgan and a British force commanded by Lieutenant-Colonel Banastre Tarleton at Cowpens on January 17, 1781 was critical for American fortunes in the South. 1780 had been the darkest of years for the American patriots. After a series of dramatic battlefield reverses which left the British in control of major economic centers and coastal seaports at Charleston and Savannah, and American armies scattered and disorganized, prospects for restoring American control over the Carolinas seemed dim. As the events of 1780 unfolded the 7th Royal Fusiliers and Delaware Continentals played critical roles in the campaign that saw them facing each other at Cowpens on a cold winter morning in January 1781.

In response to the British threat to Charleston, Washington dispatched Major General Baron Johann DeKalb with the Maryland Division to relieve

Siege of Charleston (1862), an engraving by Alonzo Chappel (1828–87). Responding to the directive from Lord George Germain to shift the focus of the war to the South, in February 1780 the British landed an expeditionary force led by overall British commander General Sir Henry Clinton in South Carolina and quickly surrounded the strategic seaport of Charleston. The 7th Royal Fusiliers, numbering 463 men, sailed south with Clinton. On May 11, 1780 Major General Benjamin Lincoln surrendered the city and approximately 5,700 American defenders, including 2,500 Continentals; this loss of manpower, arms, and supplies had a crippling effect on the American defense of the South. Following his capture of Charleston Clinton returned to New York, leaving Cornwallis to complete the task of securing first South Carolina and then the entire region. (ASKB)

Published in 1875, this lithograph depicts the death of DeKalb at the battle of Camden. On August 14, 1780 Gates approached Camden with approximately 3,000 men. Unknown to Gates, Cornwallis had arrived the previous day with reinforcements for Lieutenant-Colonel Francis Rawdon's small force defending the town. During the early morning of August 15, 1780 Gates's force stumbled into the British army. Despite misgivings on the part of DeKalb and other veteran Continental officers, the Americans decided to fight; the militia failed to stand against the initial British attack, allowing DeKalb and his Continentals to be surrounded and overwhelmed. Despite putting up a gallant defense DeKalb died in the fighting and the remnants of the Maryland brigades were scattered and retreated as best they could. (ASKB)

the besieged garrison. When the Maryland Division, organized in two brigades and composed of 1,400 Maryland and Delaware Continentals, began its march from Morristown in April 1780 the 1st Delaware Regiment headed south with 306 men in eight companies. News of the surrender of Charleston reached DeKalb on June 6, 1780 and the 1st Maryland Brigade remained near Hillsborough, North Carolina for several weeks. On June 13 following the loss of Charleston, the American Congress appointed Major General Horatio Gates the new commander of the Southern Department and dispatched him to take command of the reinforced Southern Army to challenge British control. Gates joined DeKalb at Hollingsworth Farm on the Deep River on July 25, 1780. Against the advice of his officers Gates pushed into South Carolina towards Camden along a route bereft of adequate supplies. The army, already suffering from its march at the height of the Carolina summer, was further debilitated by lack of food.

Following defeat at Camden, in early September 1780 the remains of Gates's army reassembled in Hillsborough, North Carolina, numbering slightly more than 700 men. The two Maryland brigades were amalgamated into two battalions: the remains of the 1st, 3rd, 5th, and 7th Maryland regiments composed the 1st Battalion, while the 2nd, 4th, and 6th, with the Delaware survivors, were organized as the 2nd Battalion. Both battalions were placed under the overall command of Colonel Otho Holland Williams and his deputy, Lieutenant Colonel John Eager Howard. The early-October roster for the Delaware contingent was approximately 180 men, reorganized into two companies of 90 men each. Gates further reorganized his small army in October, drawing men from the Maryland, Delaware, and Virginia Continentals to form three companies of light infantry; Captain Robert Kirkwood's 3rd Company was composed primarily of men from the 1st Delaware Regiment. Colonel Daniel Morgan, who would be promoted to brigadier general on October 13, took command of the light troops on October 2. Lieutenant Caleb Bennett of Kirkwood's company later wrote, "we found ourselves in a most deplorable situation, without arms, ammunition, baggage and little sustenance ..." (quoted in Ward 1941: 358), although Morgan's light companies apparently received priority in the distribution of needed clothes and arms. On October 8 Kirkwood's company marched with Morgan to operate in conjunction with North Carolina militia while the other Delaware company, under Captain Peter Jaquette, remained with the main army.

General Nathanael Greene was appointed new commander of the Southern Department by the Continental Congress on October 31, 1780, and assumed command at Charlotte, North Carolina on December 2. After surveying the state of the Patriot forces Greene concluded he could not move directly against

Cornwallis. On December 21 he detached Morgan with 600 men to operate in conjunction with Sumter's partisans west of the Broad River, where Morgan could draw adequate supplies and stiffen local resistance to the British. Greene explained his strategy to Washington in a letter of December 28:

> I am well satisfied with the movement, for it has answered thus far all the purposes for which I intended it. It makes the most of my inferior force, for it compels my adversary to divide his, and hold him in doubt as to his own line of conduct. He cannot leave Morgan behind him to come at me or his posts at Ninety Six or Augusta would be exposed. And he cannot chase Morgan far, or prosecute his views upon Virginia, while I am here with the country open before me. (Quoted in Johnson 1822: 340)

After suffering one man killed and two wounded during the siege of the city the 7th Royal Fusiliers formed part of the garrison of Charleston after the American surrender. Although the Fusiliers remained in Charleston for the remainder of 1780, "the Regiment was not in the highest state of efficiency; it had suffered heavily from disease and the few men that represented it were almost entirely recruits" (quoted in Cannon 1851: 90). A force of about 100 recruits destined for the 7th Royal Fusiliers had formed part of a larger detachment ambushed by Colonel Francis Marion's partisan troops in December; the British force only escaped after abandoning their baggage. In early January Cornwallis ordered the 7th Royal Fusiliers, by this time numbering 176 men under the command of Major Timothy Newmarsh, to reinforce the garrison at Ninety-Six. Along with a detachment of the 17th Light Dragoons, the regiment was then assigned to support Tarleton's pursuit of Morgan.

On January 1, 1781 Cornwallis had dispatched Lieutenant-Colonel Banastre Tarleton, leading the British Legion and the 71st (Highland) Regiment, to move along the east bank of the Broad River to flush Morgan out over King's Mountain, South Carolina, where Cornwallis would close the trap on the Patriots. Tarleton's movements did cause Morgan to retreat, but weather delayed Cornwallis's departure and Morgan escaped the trap. Despite this failure Tarleton continued to push Morgan north and west. On January 4, 1781 Tarleton, pausing at Brooke's Bush River Plantation, requested additional troops and baggage from Cornwallis. Having escorted a supply train containing four days' rations to Tarleton's encampment, the 7th Royal Fusiliers and a detachment of the 17th Light Dragoons joined Tarleton's force and the British commander continued his pursuit of Morgan.

For the next 12 days Tarleton chased Morgan, who kept just out of his reach. Tarleton rested his exhausted men at one of Morgan's abandoned encampments on January 16, 1780. Morgan, for his part, resolved to turn and confront his pursuer. He spent the early part of January 16 surveying the ground at Cowpens, South Carolina while units of militia continued to assemble. Morgan knew continuing his retreat over the Broad River would result in the loss of the bulk of the South Carolina militia. He also knew that his men were growing weary of the retreat and if Tarleton caught him and forced a fight without proper preparation he would be at a distinct disadvantage. Satisfied the ground at Cowpens favored his small army, Morgan decided to make his stand, remarking to his aide, "Captain, here is Morgan's grave or victory" (quoted in Trammel 1832: 2).

MAP KEY

1 0745hrs: The British deploy their main battleline and begin to advance. The American skirmishers fall back slowly and join the main militia line. The Little River Regiment, deployed in advance of the main militia line, slowly retires, allowing the retreating skirmishers to move through the gap.

2 0800hrs: British forces engage the American militia line. The British Legion infantry and the light infantry are hit by massed militia volley fire.

3 0805hrs: The British Legion infantry and light infantry charge the militia line, forcing it to retire.

4 0810hrs: The American militia retires through the Continental line to re-form in a pre-designated area. The British battle line approaches the Continental line and halts to re-form.

5 0815hrs: The British line advances and engages the Continental line in a brisk exchange of volleys. Lieutenant Henry Nettles' troop of the British 17th Light Dragoons attacks militia in the process of re-forming.

6 0817hrs: Colonel William Washington's Light Dragoons countercharge and drive off Nettles' troop.

7 0819hrs: Major Arthur MacArthur's 71st (Highland) Regiment and Captain David Ogilvie's troop of Legion cavalry are ordered to advance. Elements of the 71st and Ogilvie's troop move forward and scatter skirmishers of Colonel Joseph McDowell's militia and Captain Henry Connelly's North Carolina State troops.

8 0820hrs: Washington's Light Dragoons re-form.

9 0821hrs: The 71st (Highland) Regiment begins to advance against Captain Andrew Wallace's company of Virginia Continentals, holding the end of the American right flank.

10 0821hrs: Ogilvie's troop of Legion cavalry moves around the right of the American line and into its rear.

11 0822hrs: Washington's cavalry charges Ogilvie's Legion cavalry, driving them off with losses.

12 0824hrs: In response to the advance of the 71st (Highland) Regiment, Lieutenant Colonel Howard orders Wallace's Virginia company to refuse their flank. Wallace misinterprets the order and begins a retrograde movement as the 71st fires a volley. Captain John Lawson of the adjacent Virginia State company is killed and his men follow Wallace's in a retrograde movement. Seeing this, adjacent units also begin to retire. The 7th Royal Fusiliers, light infantry, and Legion infantry begin a disordered advance against the retiring Americans.

13 0827hrs: Wallace's and Lawson's Virginia companies retire, pursued by the 71st (Highland) Regiment. As the Americans reach a spot designated by Morgan they turn to face their British pursuers. Howard receives a message from Washington urging him to charge. The Continental line delivers a rolling volley into the 71st (Highland) Regiment and the 7th Royal Fusiliers.

14 0829hrs: American Continentals charge the 71st (Highland) Regiment and 7th Royal Fusiliers while Washington's cavalry attacks the 71st from the rear and flank. Colonel Andrew Pickens and the American militia return to the Continental line and fire into the disorganized 71st.

15 0833hrs: The 71st (Highland) Regiment breaks and Howard orders a general charge by the Continental line and militia, which overruns the 7th Royal Fusiliers and the British artillery.

16 0835hrs: Militia on American left flank engage the British light infantry, forcing their surrender.

17 0836hrs: Ordered to retake the guns, only a portion of the British Legion cavalry reserve responds, engaging Washington's cavalry and the Continental line before retiring. The 71st (Highland) Regiment is surrounded and surrenders. At 0840hrs Tarleton orders his surviving units to retreat.

Battlefield environment

Situated approximately 5 miles south of the Broad River, the Cowpens battlefield was bisected by the Green River Road, a dirt track. The battlefield is generally level, with changes in elevation no greater than 20ft at any one point, and varies from its highest to lowest point by no more than 45ft. As the British advanced from the south their left flank encountered a low wet area located on the American right flank, west of the Green River Road. Between the American main line and Morgan's Hill the ground dipped into a swale. Morgan's Hill provided an almost unobstructed view of the entire battlefield and would serve as a rallying point for militia. Tree cover varied throughout the battlefield. The American militia skirmishers would deploy beyond the first militia line in fields given over to young pine trees. Behind the skirmishers the tree cover was sporadic, but thicker in the area of the main Continental deployment. While trees were scattered throughout the battlefield there was little or no undergrowth. An officer who visited the battlefield afterwards wrote "I can say it would not have been my choice. In the first place, it was even enough to make race-paths, covered with a small growth of middling trees, open without underwood, and nothing to defend either in front, rear, or flank" (quoted in Williams 1943: 9).

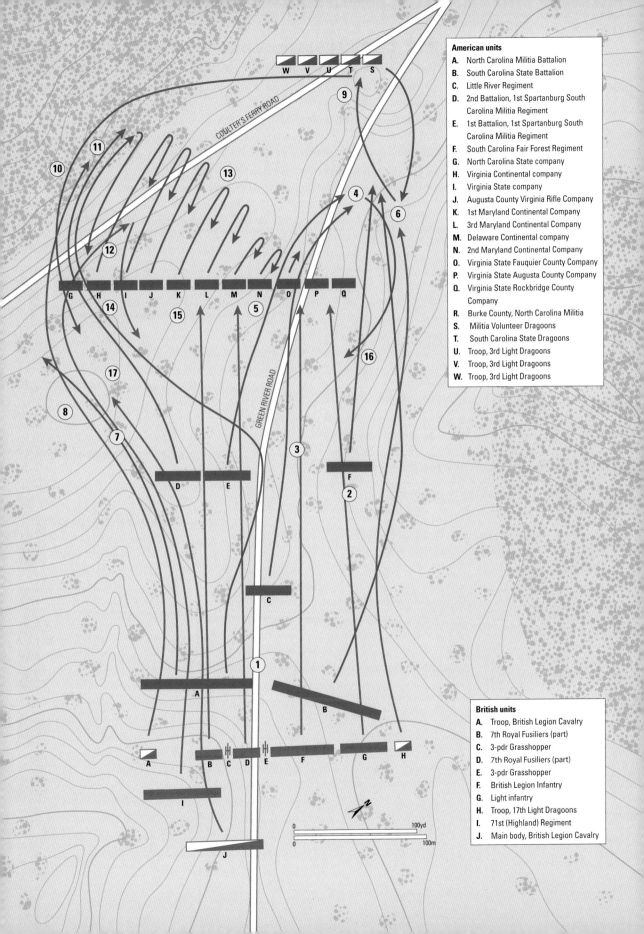

American units

A. North Carolina Militia Battalion
B. South Carolina State Battalion
C. Little River Regiment
D. 2nd Battalion, 1st Spartanburg South Carolina Militia Regiment
E. 1st Battalion, 1st Spartanburg South Carolina Militia Regiment
F. South Carolina Fair Forest Regiment
G. North Carolina State company
H. Virginia Continental company
I. Virginia State company
J. Augusta County Virginia Rifle Company
K. 1st Maryland Continental Company
L. 3rd Maryland Continental Company
M. Delaware Continental company
N. 2nd Maryland Continental Company
O. Virginia State Fauquier County Company
P. Virginia State Augusta County Company
Q. Virginia State Rockbridge County Company
R. Burke County, North Carolina Militia
S. Militia Volunteer Dragoons
T. South Carolina State Dragoons
U. Troop, 3rd Light Dragoons
V. Troop, 3rd Light Dragoons
W. Troop, 3rd Light Dragoons

COULTER'S FERRY ROAD

GREEN RIVER ROAD

British units

A. Troop, British Legion Cavalry
B. 7th Royal Fusiliers (part)
C. 3-pdr Grasshopper
D. 7th Royal Fusiliers (part)
E. 3-pdr Grasshopper
F. British Legion Infantry
G. Light infantry
H. Troop, 17th Light Dragoons
I. 71st (Highland) Regiment
J. Main body, British Legion Cavalry

0   100yd
0   100m

INTO COMBAT

Throughout the preceding day and into that night militia units from Virginia, North Carolina, and Georgia made their way into Morgan's camp. Lieutenant Colonel Howard, commanding the Continental contingent which arrived on the Cowpens battlefield during the afternoon of January 16, later remarked "that parties were coming in most of the night, and calling on Morgan for ammunition and to know the state of affairs" (quoted in Lee 1869: 226). The militia units varied in size, ranging from 100 to 300 men, organized in companies of 20–40 men. Companies and regiments were merged when necessary to achieve greater command and control.

Once the decision had been made to stand at Cowpens, Morgan assembled the commanders of his militia and Continentals after nightfall and briefed them on their expected roles. Commanders of individual regiments were assigned their place in the militia line and told what was expected of their men during the coming battle. Although ostensibly Colonel Andrew Pickens was overall commander of the militia contingent, individual commanders would be forced to make decisions for their units as the battle unfolded. Morgan moved among the militia units providing words of encouragement. Thomas Young, a South Carolina militiaman who served as a mounted trooper in Major Benjamin Jolly's troop of volunteer militia cavalry, wrote that Morgan spent the night moving among militia units are they arrived on the battlefield, telling them, "Just hold up your heads, boys, three fires and you are free and then when you return to your homes, how the old folks will bless you and the girls kiss you, for your gallant conduct" (quoted in Young 1843: 2). Morgan also provided clear instructions on how the militia should retire behind the more reliable Continental line.

At 0200hrs Tarleton dispatched his light infantry to begin a tentative advance, followed by the main British force at 0300hrs. The light-infantry companies were supported by the Legion infantry, followed by the 7th Royal Fusiliers, the 71st (Highland) Regiment, and two 3-pdr "grasshopper" light artillery pieces. The cavalry and some mounted infantry brought up the rear. The baggage wagons were left behind under a small guard. After struggling through ravines and across several creeks the British noted the appearance of a small force of militia above Macedonia Creek at 0330hrs. For his part, Morgan received regular reports from the militia outposts detailing the progress of the British throughout the early morning. The American forces were in position by 0530hrs. Morgan's scouts reported the British less than 5 miles from Cowpens one hour before daylight. Sunrise was at 0736hrs. The morning dawned with a hazy sky, temperatures below freezing and high humidity combining with a slight wind to chill the American troops waiting for the British. American militia skirmishers were deployed among the young pines, 150yd in front of Pickens' militia line. Protecting Pickens' right was the low ground of the rivulet and a line of low brush, with his men deployed along higher ground immediately behind. Pickens' left, east of the road, was on open, flatter ground.

The main line of American resistance was composed of a mix of Virginia, Maryland, North Carolina, and Delaware Continentals, North Carolina and Virginia State troops, and Virginia militia. The Continentals formed the core of Morgan's army and were deployed across the Green River Road along high ground just south of the swale and Morgan's Hill. The Continentals with

Morgan's army had all served at least a year, with most having served four or more years. Their officers were battle-tested veterans, having served through various campaigns dating back to 1775. Morgan's Continental line was organized under three commanders, all under the overall command of Lieutenant Colonel Howard.

On the American right, Captain Edmund Tate commanded a mixed group of four companies, including North Carolina State troops, Virginia Continentals, Virginia State troops, and a company of Virginia riflemen from Augusta County. The left flank was defended by three companies of Virginia militia and a single company of North Carolina militia, all under the command of Major Frank Triplett. In the center three companies of Maryland Continentals, composed of remnants of seven Maryland regiments, deployed along with Kirkwood's Delaware company. Kirkwood's 60 Continental veterans silently listened as the sounds of battle to their front grew louder. They shifted nervously in the cold January chill and waited to meet the British regulars surging towards their line.

As Tarleton's dragoons pushed forward the militia, skirmishers fell back towards the first militia line. British infantry, marching up the Green River Road, dropped packs and blankets and began to deploy for battle. The British Legion infantry and light infantry moved to the east of the road, while the 7th Royal Fusiliers formed line on the left, their right flank anchored by one 3-pdr cannon on the Green River Road while a second cannon was deployed farther to the left as part of the Fusiliers' line. The 71st (Highland) Regiment was initially ordered to remain 150yd behind the 7th Royal Fusiliers and extend its line farther to the left. Both flanks were secured by troops of British Legion cavalry.

As the British line advanced and passed the wet ground around the rivulet, Tarleton ordered the Highlanders to move up and extend the British line farther to the left of the 7th Royal Fusiliers. As the men of the 71st moved to execute the order they found the ground constrained by a ravine, restricting the ability of the troop of light dragoons to extend their line and make room for the Highlanders. As a result, the right of the 71st (Highland) Regiment's line became intermixed with the extreme left of the 7th Royal Fusiliers, causing considerable disorder. Some of the inexperienced men of the Fusiliers added to the confusion by nervously discharging their muskets before Major Newmarsh could restore order. As Tarleton later wrote, "the troops moved on in as good a line as troops could move at open files" (Tarleton 1787: 223).

As the British advanced towards the militia skirmish line, the Americans kept up a steady and galling fire. McDowell's men concentrated their fire on the Fusiliers as they advanced steadily, falling back only when "the bayonet was presented" (Tarleton 1787: 223). The skirmishers retired towards the militia line, filing through gaps between the units and then resuming their fire. Tarleton urged his men to advance at the quick step and as they crested a small ridge the British were confronted with the main line of militia. While the British Legion infantry and light infantry on the right moved quickly, the Fusiliers were delayed as Newmarsh restored order after the interpenetration of the 71st (Highland) Regiment and then sought to suppress the jittery musket fire. The two British cannon kept up a steady fire at a range of approximately 200yd but, due to the positioning of the militia below the crest of the ridge, most of the balls overshot their targets.

Published in the *Hibernian Magazine* in 1776, this engraving depicts a "real American rifle man." American militia, armed with rifles, formed Brigadier General Daniel Morgan's first two lines of defense at Cowpens. Although the British pushed through both lines, the riflemen inflicted casualties and continued to harass them from the flanks as the British approached the main line of Continental troops. (ASKB)

As the British began their advance against the militia line, several accounts noted they gave three loud cheers in an attempt to intimidate the militia. Lieutenant Thomas Anderson of the Delaware company later wrote in his journal "… about Sunrise they began the attack by the Discharge of two pieces of Cannon and three Huzzas advancing briskly on Our riflemen …" (quoted in Dawson 1867: 209). Morgan, who was moving along the militia line offering words of encouragement and support, responded by yelling, "they give us the British halloo, boys, give them the Indian halloo, by G__" (quoted in Young 1843: 3). Morgan, assisted by the regimental officers, also encouraged the militia to hold their fire, admonishing them to fire "low and deliberately" (quoted in Ward 1941: 374). The British crested the ridge advancing "at sort of a trot" (Seymour 1883: 294) while the militia waited at the edge of a treeline. The American militia fire began on their left, against the British Legion and light infantry who had moved in advance of the Fusiliers. At roughly 30yd the militia line blazed orange in the early-morning light. Although staggered, the Legion and light infantry continued their advance, absorbing a second volley as they tried to rally. Twice the British light infantry attempted a bayonet charge only to be stopped by the American fire. Return fire from the Legion and light infantry was largely ineffective, in part due to the militia deployment on the reverse slope, which caused the British to fire high. Recovering quickly from the initial militia volley, the Legion Infantry charged forward, causing the riflemen – without bayonets and unable to reload – to flee.

With their left retreating, the militia battalions on the American right, opposite the 7th Royal Fusiliers, also retired. As Sergeant Major William Seymour of Kirkwood's Delaware company observed, "the enemy advanced and attacked the militia in front, which they stood very well for some time … they retreated, but in very good order, not seeming to be in the least confused" (Seymour 1883: 294). Because the men of the 7th Royal Fusiliers had lagged behind the advance of the Legion and light infantry they were spared the destructive militia volley. The American militia line retired, as Morgan had planned, in good order to either side of the Continental line to re-form.

Some 150yd behind the militia line, partially hidden by thicker woods, Morgan's Continentals waited for the British. After the initial militia volley Morgan had moved back to the Continental line and along with

The ground east of the Green River Road was generally more open than the area west of the road. It was in this area that the British light infantry deployed after dispersing the first militia line. (Author)

The British light infantry pushed the militia riflemen of the first American line back towards the second line. As the light infantry inclined to the right and deployed east of the Green River Road, the 7th Royal Fusiliers deployed west of the road. This photo looks toward the second American line. (Author)

Lieutenant Colonel Howard assured the Maryland and Delaware veterans that the militia retreat was to be expected. As Private Henry Wells of Kirkwood's Delaware company remembered, "at the outset we were much alarmed by the Superiority of the Enemy in numbers, but the powerful & trumpet like voice of our Commander drove fear from every bosom, and gave new energies to every arm" (Wells 1834).

The soldiers in the British line, having marched throughout the early morning across difficult terrain, then advancing at a quick pace through the steady fire from first the American skirmishers, then the militia line, stopped to re-form; Lieutenant Anderson recounted "… the Enemy, Seeing us Standing in Such good Order Halted for Some time to dress their line Which outflanked ours considerably" (quoted in Dawson 1867: 209). Thinking that they had routed the Americans and all that was left was to disperse any remaining militia, the British were now faced by a solid line of veteran American Continentals. The Legion infantry and light infantry, re-formed from open order to a two-rank line, shortened their line to avoid a wet area that would have slowed their advance protecting the American left flank. The 7th Royal Fusiliers, moving up on the British left, deployed with their right flank on the road, anchored by a 3-pdr cannon, while the other gun continued to be located in the center of their line. Although the Fusiliers had been spared the devastating volley from the militia, they had advanced under a constant hail of rifle fire, which had killed and wounded scores of men. The 71st (Highland) Regiment, still to the rear and left of the 7th Royal Fusiliers, struggled to extend the British line on the left.

As the British dressed their lines the militia riflemen filtered through the Continental line on the right and kept up a desultory fire. With their lines re-formed, the British pushed forward toward the Continentals. As they advanced, Howard's line erupted in a sustained sequence of volleys. Owing to their deployment the Legion and light infantry squared off against Triplett's Virginia battalion, while the Fusiliers advanced opposite the Maryland and Delaware Continentals in the center of the Continental line. Because they overlapped the British line, the men of Tate's battalion on the American right concentrated their fire into the 7th Royal Fusiliers. Adding to the Fusiliers' discomfort were the swarms of militia still hovering around the British flank.

1782

1782

1782

As casualties mounted, the 7th Royal Fusiliers closed ranks by collapsing towards the single 3-pdr cannon, located in the center of their line, directly opposite Kirkwood's Delaware company.

Morgan's report to Greene noted that "when the enemy advanced on our lines they received a well directed and incessant fire" (Myers 1881: 25). Other recollections stated the fire "was kept up with coolness and constancy" (quoted in Ward 1941: 374). Howard had organized a sequence of fire for each of his three battalions, designating one company in each to fire in turn so that when one company was firing another was reloading, and a third had already loaded and was ready to fire. As Thomas Young recounted, "when the regulars fired, it seemed like one sheet of flame from right to left" (Young 1843: 100). Historian Henry Lee later wrote that "Tarleton pushed forward and was received by his adversary with unshaken firmness. The contest became obstinate; each party, animated by the example of its leader, nobly contended for victory" (Lee 1869: 228). Both Morgan and Tarleton were conspicuous by their presence as the firefight raged. Howard also rode along his line, encouraging the Continentals to stand firm.

Tarleton could see his regulars were stymied: "the contest between the British infantry in the front and the continentals seemed equally balanced, neither retreating" (Tarleton 1787: 223). To break the deadlock Tarleton ordered the Highlanders to move up on the British left and add their weight to the fight. He also ordered the Legion cavalry on each flank to engage the Americans. On the British right the Legion cavalry attacked the re-forming militia in the swale, throwing them momentarily into panic before Lieutenant Colonel William Washington's Light Dragoons drove the British horsemen off. On the British left, Ogilvie's troop of Legion cavalry charged through McDowell's skirmishers, driving them farther back into Maple Swamp, from where they continued to pepper the cavalry and the 71st (Highland) Regiment. The 71st rushed forward in column, with one or two companies deployed in line, followed by the Legion Cavalry reserve. Tarleton later recounted that as they advanced the Highlanders deployed into line, and "the 71st were desired to pass the 7th before they gave their fire and were directed not to entangle their right flank with the left of the other battalion" (Tarleton 1787: 223).

Howard recognized the intent of the British movement and issued orders to Captain Andrew Wallace's company of Virginia Continentals, holding the extreme right of the line, to refuse their flank to face the advancing Highlanders. Whether the wrong order was delivered or simply misunderstood either by Wallace or his men, rather than refuse the flank, the Virginians turned and began to march away. At the same time the Highlanders, who had advanced to about 40yd of Tate's line, delivered a deadly volley into the Continental line. Immediately to the left of Wallace's company, Captain John Lawson's Virginia State company was thrown into confusion by the death of its commander. Lieutenant Thomas Taylor assumed command and, seeing Wallace's Continental company marching away, now ordered his company to follow suit. In succession, the remaining Continental companies assumed a general order to retire had been given, and also faced about. Each company, as their neighboring company retired, followed in turn. Seymour noted that "Captain Kirkwood with his company wheeled to the right" (Seymour 1883: 294), while Virginian Private John Thomas observed that Kirkwood's Delaware company "fired before they retreated" (Thomas 1832). As the line performed its staggered movement a surprised Morgan confronted Howard, demanding a reason for the retreat and asking if his men were beaten. Howard responded, "Do men who march like that look as though they are beaten?" (quoted in Ward 1941: 377). Reassured, Morgan pointed out a spot on rising ground and ordered Howard to halt his men at that point and deliver a volley.

Seeing the American line retiring and the Continentals turning their back to them, first the 71st (Highland) Regiment and then the 7th Royal Fusiliers began spontaneously to advance. The British had been marching since 0300hrs, moving forward in the cold early morning through ravines and across small streams. The *History of the 7th Royal Fusiliers* noted that "it was about 8 a.m. when Tarleton commenced his attack, and his troops, having been five hours on the march were greatly fatigued" (Groves 1903: 93). After being disorganized early in the battle by the accidental interpenetration of the 71st (Highland) Regiment the Fusiliers suffered casualties from the concentrated volleys of the American militia line. As they advanced they continued to be discomforted by continual sniping from the militia skirmishers on their flank. The physical and psychological toll on the 7th Royal Fusiliers, many of whom had relatively little battlefield experience, began to impact upon their cohesion and discipline.

As Tarleton simply reported, "the British rushed forward" (Tarleton 1787: 223). Lieutenant Anderson noted the 7th Royal Fusiliers, "thinking that We Were broke set up a great Shout Charged us With their bayonets but in no Order" (quoted in Dawson 1867: 209). The British pursuit was also hampered by the somewhat dense tree coverage. Wallace's company retired approximately 100yd in about 90 seconds, before turning about, followed closely by the Highlanders. The other Continental companies retired some 80–100yd, reloading as they moved, coming into line with Wallace's Continental company. First Wallace's men and then the other Continental companies turned and fired a volley in sequence. The movement of the Continentals conformed closely to Steuben's training manual.

Howard later related that "as soon as the word was given to halt and face about the line was perfectly formed in a moment. The enemy pressed upon us in rather disorder, expecting the fate of the day was decided. They were by this time within 30 yards of us … my men with uncommon coolness gave them an unexpected and deadly fire" (Lee 1824: 96). As Howard was designating the spot for Wallace's company to halt, a messenger from Lieutenant Colonel Washington rode up and reported Washington had taken note of the British pursuit: "they are coming on like a mob. Give them a fire and I will charge them" (quoted in

Dating from 1916, these details from a watercolor by Richard Simkin (1840–1926) show personnel of the 7th Royal Fusiliers in full-dress uniforms in 1782 – a far cry from campaign garb. By January 1781 the appearance of the 7th Royal Fusiliers, like most of the British units operating in the South, had been impacted by the combination of local conditions and lack of resupply. After suffering the hardships of Tarleton's pursuit through the Carolina backcountry, many of the uniforms would have been patched and soiled. Some of the men would have traded their cocked hats for large round hats, perhaps turned up on one side or the back. Most of the men would have also carried blanket rolls since Tarleton's baggage train was reduced to a bare minimum to improve mobility, although these and backpacks were shed prior to engaging in combat. (ASKB)

This watercolor of 1780 shows Highlanders rescuing a wounded officer in battle. Lieutenant Robert Mackenzie, serving with the 71st (Highland) Regiment at Cowpens, wrote that as the British infantry continued their advance towards the retreating Continental line "a number, not less than two-thirds of the British infantry officers, had already fallen, and nearly the same proportion of privates; fatigue, however, enfeebled the pursuit, much more than loss of blood" (Mackenzie 1789: 99). (ASKB)

Robert Kirkwood

Born in Newark, Delaware, in 1756, Robert Kirkwood was named a lieutenant in Colonel John Haslet's Regiment of Continentals in 1776 and fought at Long Island and other major engagements throughout that year. Haslett's Regiment, reduced by casualties and expiration of enlistments, was re-formed as the 1st Delaware Regiment and Kirkwood was promoted to captain of the 2nd Company in December 1776. Detached on a recruiting mission, Kirkwood missed the battles of Trenton and Princeton, but fought at the battles of Brandywine in September and Germantown in October 1777. Later in 1777 Kirkwood was furloughed, but returned to the army in 1779.

Kirkwood and the 1st Delaware Regiment fought at Camden, suffering horrific casualties which reduced the regiment to two companies. In October 1780 Kirkwood was appointed commander of one company, reinforced with Maryland troops, and in December, Major General Greene detached Kirkwood to operate with Brigadier General Morgan. Although part of the larger army, the Delaware company operated largely as an independent unit and was assigned a variety of roles. While Kirkwood was only a captain, the welfare of his men required him to assume responsibilities usually expected of officers of higher rank.

At Cowpens Kirkwood was nominally under command of Lieutenant Colonel Howard but was expected to exercise complete control over his company. When the companies to his right began their retrograde movement, Kirkwood, understanding that unless his company conformed to their action he would expose his right flank to attack from the 71st (Highland) Regiment, also ordered a retirement. After playing a key role at Cowpens, Kirkwood and his Delaware company fought at Guilford Courthouse (March 15, 1781). Kirkwood fought under Greene's command throughout the 1781 Southern campaign and in January 1782 was furloughed back to Delaware. At the close of the war, Kirkwood was brevetted major. He later moved to the North West Territory and in 1791, aged 35, was killed in a battle with warriors from the Miami tribe at Fort Recovery, near the border of the present-day states of Indiana and Ohio.

This 1834 engraving shows John Eager Howard, who commanded the Continental line at Cowpens. Lieutenant Colonel Howard was a veteran of previous campaigns and had a reputation as an excellent officer, commanding Maryland troops. (Library of Congress)

Johnson 1822: 381). Washington's cavalry had formed Morgan's reserve deployed behind Morgan's Hill, and had already averted a catastrophe by driving off Ogilvie's troop of Legion cavalry that had swept through the American militia skirmishers and threatened the rear of Howard's line.

The Continental line gave "a close and murderous fire" to the 71st (Highland) Regiment, and "nearly one half of their number fell" (Stewart 1825: 139). Surprised by the sudden volley from the Continentals, some British soldiers "threw down their arms and fell upon their faces," while the remainder were scattered in disorder; "Exertions to make them advance were useless [and] an unaccountable panic extended itself along the whole line" (Shaw 1807: 54–55). Seeing the 71st halted and in disorder, Morgan recalled, Howard "gave orders for the line to charge bayonets, which was done with such address that the enemy fled …" (quoted in Myers 1881: 24–25). Lieutenant Anderson recounted the "Americans were in amongst them with bayonets which caused them to give ground and at last to take flight" (Dawson 1867: 209). Washington's cavalry, forming behind Howard's line, swept into the Highlanders on the heels of the American volley. Despite the Highlanders' disorganization the 71st resisted the American advance, engaging the Virginia and Maryland Continentals with bayonets and an occasional musket shot. Adding to the circle tightening around the Highlanders the main body of American militia, now reorganized, surged over Morgan's Hill and peppered the Scots with incessant fire, while McDowell's militia crept out of Maple Swamp to complete the encirclement. "We let them come within ten or fifteen yards of us then give them a full volley and at the same time charged them home. They not expecting any such thing put them in such confusion that we were in amongst them with the bayonets …" (quoted in Dawson 1867: 209).

Moses Bright

Born in 1736 in Newbury, Berkshire, Moses Bright enlisted aged 34 in the 62nd Regiment of Foot in January 1770. After serving with his regiment in Ireland, Bright and the 62nd Regiment sailed to Canada in early 1776. Bright was wounded in action during the Saratoga campaign in 1777 and taken prisoner. After some time in captivity Bright escaped and was assigned to the 7th Royal Fusiliers in December 1778. Wounded again during the British raids against Fairfield and Norwalk, Connecticut in 1779, Bright was promoted to corporal in July 1778 and rejoined the 7th Royal Fusiliers in time to sail south in early 1780 with the British task force that captured Charleston, South Carolina.

Bright served throughout 1780 in the campaign across South Carolina, marching with the 7th Royal Fusiliers to the battlefield at Cowpens. As a seasoned veteran in a regiment with a large contingent of recent recruits, Corporal Bright would have been responsible for setting an example during the rigors on combat for the men under his command. In the aftermath of the confusion caused by interpenetration of the 71st (Highland) Regiment with the 7th Royal Fusiliers, Corporal Bright would have been responsible for restoring order and ending the premature firing of muskets by the jittery privates. As casualties mounted, particularly among officers, Corporal Bright assisted in dressing the ranks as the regiment prepared to assault the Continental line. Bright survived the battle of Cowpens unharmed, but was captured along with most of his companions.

Corporal Bright escaped again and rejoined the remnants of the 7th Royal Fusiliers in Savannah, Georgia. He was promoted to sergeant and ended the war in New York in 1782, from where the 7th Royal Fusiliers were transported back to England the following year. With the reduction in force following the war, Bright choose to obtain his discharge. In 1797 Bright petitioned the commissioners of Chelsea Hospital for an out-pension and apparently served in the invalid company of two British costal garrisons, being later discharged from service in 1804.

> … the Highlanders, who now saw no prospect of support, while their own numbers were diminishing and the enemy increasing. They began to retire and at length to run, the first instance of a Highland regiment running from an enemy. This retreat struck a panic into those whom they left in the rear, who fled in the greatest confusion: order and command were lost; the rout became general … (Stewart 1825: 139–40)

In the center Kirkwood's Delaware company promptly surged forward into the reeling ranks of the 7th Royal Fusiliers, causing the British soldiers to surrender after a brief melee. Unlike their battlefield opponents, the men of the Delaware company had enjoyed a relatively restful night, eaten a quick breakfast and spent the morning deployed in place. Although suffering from the freezing temperatures they had not been fatigued from constant motion prior to engaging in combat. From their position they could hear the sounds of the battle as it moved toward them and were not surprised when the masses of militia retired around their flanks. All were experienced veterans and knew what to expect once the British line began its advance against them. Rather than being disoriented by the unexpected order to retire, they deliberately responded as trained. Having arrived at the spot designated by Howard in good order, they obeyed Captain Robert Smallwood's command to turn and fire. Howard urged his men to capture the two 3-pdr cannon, still manned and ready to fire. Lieutenant Thomas Anderson and men from Kirkwood's Delaware company cut down the crew of one of the guns opposite their position, while men from Captain Richard Anderson's 1st Maryland Continental Company captured the other. Tarleton, seeing the Highlanders and Royal Fusiliers disintegrating and the cannon overrun, ordered his Legion cavalry reserve to counterattack. Although several

Continental counterattack

After a grueling night march and fighting their way through two lines of American militia the British approached the Continental line. The unintended retirement of several Continental companies on the right of the American line resulted in the disordered pursuit by the British 71st (Highland) Regiment and 7th Royal Fusiliers. The Continentals retired in good order, turning abruptly to fire a destructive volley into the pursuing British. As the British infantry recoiled from the volley the Continentals lowered their muskets and countercharged. The Delaware Continentals, deployed opposite the 7th Royal Fusiliers, are shown driving back the Fusiliers and overrunning the 3-pdr gun deployed in the center of their line. The Delaware Continentals, dressed in hunting shirts, are rushing forward; they will capture or kill the British artillery crew defending their gun and shatter the 7th Royal Fusiliers.

Published in 1858, this engraving by Alonzo Chappel (1828–87) shows the clash between Washington and Tarleton. During the course of the final charge of Lieutenant Colonel William Washington's cavalry against the disorganized British infantry, Tarleton ordered his Legion cavalry to countercharge. Many of the Legion cavalry refused to advance, but several did move forward and engage the American cavalry. Several veterans later recounted that during this melee Washington and several officers advanced forward towards the Legion command group. The Legion cavalry, which included Tarleton, promptly charged Washington and a confused fight ensued. Accounts vary as to whether Washington and Tarleton ever crossed swords but all agree that Washington, with a broken sword, was saved from harm by the timely intervention of his aide and servant and had his horse wounded by a pistol shot. Tarleton was also wounded, losing two fingers during the fight. (ASKB)

troopers responded by charging towards the British guns, they were met by a solid mass of Continental bayonets and attacked by Washington's cavalry, while the majority of the British horsemen wheeled around and retired. On the British right flank the light infantry was overwhelmed and surrendered.

Immediately after the battle Morgan ordered Kirkwood's Delaware company to support the American pursuit of Tarleton's routed force. After suffering 15 men dead and wounded, the highest percentage loss of any unit of Morgan's force, Kirkwood's men marched 12 miles alongside Washington's cavalry and various militia units, gathering up the British supply train and stragglers. The history of the 7th Royal Fusiliers recorded that "the Royal Fusiliers were, as a regiment, practically destroyed; their casualties amongst the men are not recorded but they were very heavy" (Groves 1903: 95). Other sources suggest 15 men of the regiment managed to escape. Of the nine officers present, two were killed and three, including Major Newmarsh, wounded; the regimental colors, along with the baggage, were lost.

Analysis

The British Army entered the American Revolutionary War with a distinct advantage. The army was sprinkled with veterans of the French and Indian War, including most of the top commanders. Learning from the lessons of the French and Indian War, British commander Lieutenant-General Howe developed and implemented innovative tactical doctrine for light infantry and extended it to line regiments.

The nascent army assembled under General Washington's command around Boston in 1775 was, like most revolutionary forces, infused with a

This detail of a map of the battle of Brandywine published in 1778 by William Faden, shows the area of the British flank attack and the area of the Americans' initial deployment and retreat. (Library of Congress)

NOTE *The Operations of the Column un*
the Command of His Excellar
Lieutenant General Knyphau
is engraved from a Plan dra
on the Spot by S.W. WERN
Leiut.ᵗ of Hefsian Artille
Engraved by Wᵐ FADEN
Charing Crofs,
1778.

Major General John Sullivan (1740–95) is depicted as a brigadier general in this engraving published in 1775/76. Prior to the battle of Brandywine Sullivan's combat record was mixed. He shared command of American troops on Long Island, fighting bravely on August 27, 1776 before being captured. Subsequently exchanged, Sullivan served ably under Washington's command at the battles of Trenton and Princeton. On September 11, 1777 he responded with alacrity to Washington's directive to move his division to counter the British flanking movement and to assume overall command of that threatened flank. Sullivan's division marched over unfamiliar terrain and found itself some distance from the American line forming at Birmingham Hill. In his role as overall commander Sullivan left the division to confer with Brigadier Generals Stephen and Stirling. The decision to order his division to redeploy to tie into Stephen's flank in the face of the impending British attack was ill advised and resulted in the disordering his division and the men of both Stephen's and Stirling's divisions as they shifted to make room for Sullivan's men. Despite the collapse of his division Sullivan continued to assist Stephen and Stirling in rallying their divisions. In 1778 Sullivan commanded the failed expedition with the French to capture Newport, Rhode Island and in 1779 led a successful campaign against the Iroquois in western New York. Disillusioned with the lack of recognition from Congress, Sullivan retired from the Continental Army in late 1779. (ASKB)

strong spirit of purpose and enthusiasm. Unfortunately the disparate units that assembled at Boston lacked real cohesion and – most importantly – any formal training. While some American officers brought with them battlefield experience from the French and Indian War, many were untested. Worse yet, the militia that constituted the majority of the American Army exhibited that unique American streak of independence, which while essential in succoring the spirit of revolution, did not contribute to creating an effective fighting force. The British evacuation of Boston did nothing to dampen the delusion that revolutionary ardor could more than make up for the widespread lack of disciple and training. Reality set in during 1776 as the British returned, landing in New York and outmaneuvering Washington and his Continental army in a series of defeats that highlighted the inability of American troops to stand toe to toe with their British opponents. At the same time the ease in which they were able to overwhelm the American Continentals and militia almost at will reinforced the British perception of American weakness. The 1776 campaign ended with Washington launching a desperate attack against a Hessian detachment at Trenton, New Jersey on December 26 and then outmaneuvering Howe's pursuing army and retreating to Morristown where the American Army spent the winter. Those actions revived the lagging spirit of rebellion and allowed Washington to refill his depleted ranks, reorganize and reclothe his regiments and – most importantly – conduct rudimentary training throughout the winter of 1777/78.

The battle of Brandywine provided the first test of the durability of Washington's recently reorganized and reinvigorated American Army. At Brandywine Creek Howe once again outmaneuvered Washington, but despite the confusion over Major General Sullivan's poorly chosen deployment, the Continentals defended their positions in a manner that surprised the British. Although the Americans were able to adjust on the fly to the British flanking movement and engaged the British in a lively firefight, the Guards and grenadiers drove the Americans from their positions with repeated bayonet charges. In the twilight of the early evening the 2nd Virginia Regiment, along with the rest of Brigadier General Weedon's brigade, stood their ground against the steady advance of the British grenadiers and 4th Brigade. After their initial surprise the 64th Regiment traded volleys with the 2nd Virginia until darkness ended the long day of march and countermarch.

After a long winter at Valley Forge, Washington's newly trained Continental army marched into battle at Monmouth Courthouse with a new sense of confidence. Facing the Americans was a battle-tested British army at the height of its military prowess. It is doubtful that Washington wanted to bring on a full battle in attacking the British rearguard, but Lieutenant-General Clinton's quick decision to counterattack with the cream of the British Army, the grenadiers and Guards, seized the initiative and forced the Americans back in headlong retreat. In spite of the confusion among their officers and their own disappointment at again watching their lines crumble before the British onslaught, the American Continentals conducted their retreat in a measured manner and in good order. Throughout the course of the initial advance and subsequent retreat the Continentals changed formation as needed from column to line, maneuvering around the battlefield as ordered and stopping several times to delay the British advance. Although driven back, the

An American map of the battle of Monmouth, published in 1778. "A" indicates the left wing of the British the night before; "B" indicates American troops near the courthouse; "C" indicates Lee's first position during his retreat; "D" indicates Lee's later positions; "E" indicates Lee's last position; "F" indicates the dispositions of the American force after Washington met Lee, with the asterisk showing where they met; "G" indicates the site of the principal battle; and "H" indicates the British positions after the action. (Library of Congress)

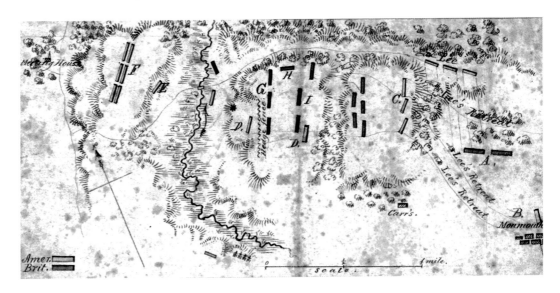

Continentals showed no panic as they had in the campaigns around New York and even at Brandywine. For their part the British grenadiers pushed forward, as they had at Brandywine, believing the Americans unable and unwilling to contest their advance. When posted to good advantage, in this case behind a substantial fence, Lieutenant Colonel Olney's 2nd Rhode Island, supported by the composite 4th and 8th Connecticut Regiment and 4th New York Regiment, were not cowed by the inextricable advance of the British grenadiers. The grenadiers, disorganized by an advance over several miles in extreme heat, buoyed by their success in driving the Americans before them and encouraged by Clinton, failed to reorder their ranks properly and were stopped by the determined resistance of Olney's men. After a short but deadly exchange of musket fire the Continentals retired across a causeway, followed by the grenadiers, whose advance was again stopped by the line of American artillery on Perrine Ridge.

As the last major battle in the north, Monmouth established a battlefield parity between the British regulars and the American Continentals. Although both sides initiated limited operations around New York, neither side was willing to risk a major battle. British policy now dictated that the seat of war move south to the Carolinas. Many of the veterans of Brandywine and Monmouth would again face each other in a different theater. In the aftermath of the loss of veteran units in the surrender of Charleston, South Carolina and the debacle at Camden, Major General Greene's army contained only a small core of Continental units. As Greene took command in December 1780 he had to depend on the questionable reliability of local militia to supplement the Continentals. Similarly, Lieutenant-General Cornwallis's British army was composed of a nucleus of experienced regulars supported by an odd assortment

of Loyalist units. By this stage in the war both British and American regiments were buttressed by infusions of new recruits.

Brigadier General Morgan's understanding of the psychology of his militia units led him to deploy them at Cowpens in a manner that maximized their effectiveness and minimized their vulnerability. He understood that to ask too much of the militia was to court disaster, as previous American commanders had learned to their detriment. The American Continentals at Cowpens were not large in number, but brought to the battle years of battlefield experience. That experience allowed them to recover from what could have been a catastrophic mistake that might have given the British a deadly advantage. By contrast, the British force commanded by Lieutenant-Colonel Tarleton included several light-infantry companies, the 71st (Highland) Regiment, and the 7th Royal Fusiliers, in addition to his own British Legion cavalry. After marching through the early morning and suffering casualties as they dispersed the first two militia lines Tarleton's men found themselves confronted by a solid line of Continentals. Fatigue and an ill-advised deployment combined to fragment the British attack. Even at that stage the American Continentals were hard pressed to maintain their position and a misunderstood order resulted in a portion of their line retreating. The veteran companies retired in good order, before turning on their British pursuers to deliver a devastating volley. Disordered and shaken by the American volley, the British regulars disintegrated under the Continental charge.

For the Americans Tarleton's loss reaffirmed the proper use of militia and Continentals, a lesson Greene used to his advantage at Guilford Courthouse in March 1781. The collapse of the British 7th Royal Fusiliers and 71st (Highland) Regiment at Cowpens not only deprived Cornwallis of two veteran units, but highlighted a new battlefield parity between British regulars and American Continentals. At Yorktown in 1781 the Hessian officer Johann Ewald, a veteran of the long war, commented that

> … the so called Continental, or standing regiments are under good discipline and drill in the English style as well as the English themselves. I have seen the Rhode Island Regiment march and perform several mountings of the guard which left nothing to criticize. The men were complete masters of their legs, carried their weapons well, held their heads straight, faced right without moving an eye, and wheeled so excellently without their officers having to shout much, that the regiment looked like it was dressed in line with a string. (Ewald 1979: 340)

Lieutenant-Colonel Banastre Tarleton is depicted in this 1782 work by J. Walker. Criticism of Tarleton's leadership at Cowpens followed almost immediately in the aftermath of his defeat. Tarleton blamed his loss on the refusal of the British Legion cavalry to charge as ordered and later included criticism of the 7th Royal Fusiliers and the widespread use of open-order formations. Acting under Tarleton's threat to resign unless exonerated, Lieutenant-General Cornwallis also placed the blame on the troops. Despite Cornwallis's excuses, it was widely suggested that Tarleton did not handle his cavalry properly, breaking it into three detachments and diluting its effectiveness. He was also charged with not concentrating his forces before ordering the attack and failing to recognize the need to immediately support his infantry in the aftermath of the Continental counterattack. After the war, Tarleton engaged in a series of acrimonious exchanges with Lieutenant Roderick Mackenzie of the 71st (Highland) Regiment, who challenged Tarleton's explanations for his defeat. (Library of Congress)

This monument was erected by Congress in 1932 to commemorate the battle of Cowpens. Designated a national battlefield site in 1929, Cowpens was given full national park designation in 1972. (Author)

Aftermath

The six regiments featured in this book experienced mixed fortunes as the conflict wore on. After Brandywine the 2nd Virginia Regiment fought with distinction at Germantown on October 4, 1777 and at Monmouth Courthouse in June 1778, but by September 1778 casualties, desertion, and expiration of enlistments reduced its strength. In 1779 the regiment furnished 61 men for a light-infantry company that were assigned to Brigadier General Wayne's Corps of Light Infantry and participated in the capture of Stony Point in July 1779 and the attack on Paulus Hook. A company of veteran Virginia Continentals fought at Cowpens in January 1780. A reconstituted 2nd Virginia Regiment joined Major General Greene's army in early 1781 and fought at Guilford Courthouse, Hobkirk's Hill, and Eutaw Springs before being disbanded in 1783.

After Brandywine the 64th Regiment fought at Germantown before joining the garrison in Philadelphia, where they were quartered until Clinton abandoned the city in June 1778. The 64th supported the British attack at Monmouth Courthouse and retired to New York with the main army. The 64th was part of the British army sent south in December 1779 and took part in the siege and capture of Charleston in April 1780. After the light and grenadier companies of the 64th were withdrawn and returned with Clinton to New York, the center companies were assigned to various posts in South Carolina, fighting at Eutaw Springs in September 1781. While the light company of the 64th surrendered with Lieutenant-General Cornwallis in October 1781 the center companies, reunited with their grenadier company, remained in Charleston until they were evacuated in December 1782.

Immediately after the battle of Monmouth Courthouse the 2nd Rhode Island Regiment assisted in burying the dead and recovering the wounded. In June 1778 the 2nd Rhode Island Regiment was dispatched to join Major General Sullivan's army in Rhode Island. After the Rhode Island campaign ended in defeat for the Americans, the 2nd Rhode Island rejoined the main American

Army and fought at the battle of Springfield in June 1780. In January 1781 the 2nd Rhode Island Regiment was merged with the 1st Rhode Island Regiment. The composite Rhode Island Regiment formed part of Washington's army at Yorktown and was finally disbanded in December 1783.

Returning to New York in early July 1778, the British 1st and 2nd Grenadier battalions had an uncertain future. Upon arriving in New York, the grenadier companies were returned to their parent regiments, much to the consternation of some of the grenadier company officers, who interpreted the disbandment of the battalions as censure for their performance at Monmouth Courthouse. Senior officers reassured the grenadiers that the move was merely an act of economy and only temporary. Although the grenadier battalions were reconstituted in late August and sent to relieve the British garrison in Rhode Island, they arrived after the Americans had retreated. The grenadier battalions participated in raids and minor expeditions around New York and New Jersey over the course of the next few years. Several of the grenadier companies rejoined their parent regiments and participated in the capture of Charleston before returning to New York in May 1780. The grenadier battalions took part in no major actions for the remainder of the war.

Captain Robert Kirkwood's Delaware company was reunited with its sister company in March 1781, and both fought at Guilford Courthouse. The Delaware Continentals remained with Major General Greene's Southern Army, fighting at Hobkirk's Hill, the siege of 96 and the battle of Eutaw Springs. Several newly recruited Delaware companies joined General Washington's army at Yorktown, while the veteran Delaware Continentals remained in the south. At the Combahee River in August 1782 the Delaware Regiment fought in the last skirmish of the war against elements of the British 64th Regiment. The Delaware Regiment returned to Delaware on January 17, 1783.

Those men of the 7th Royal Fusiliers that were able to escape the debacle at Cowpens retired to Charleston, South Carolina where they joined another detachment and assumed garrison duty for the remainder of the war. A small group of the 7th Fusiliers joined Cornwallis's army and eventually surrendered at Yorktown. The 7th Royal Fusiliers had the distinction of being the only British regiment to lose its colors twice during the course of the war.

WORKS CITED

Adams, Samuel (1778). *Samuel Adams's Private Miscellaneous Diary Ann: Dom: 1778. Kept partly in the Town of Dorchester and partly in his Excellency General Washington's Camp at Valley Forge, White Plains, Fredericksburgh, &c ...*, Samuel Adams Diaries, Manuscript Division, New York Public Library.

Agnew, Daniel (1898). "A Biographical Sketch of Governor Richard Howell, of New Jersey," in *Pennsylvania Magazine of History and Biography*, Vol. 22 No. 2. Philadelphia, PA: Historical Society of Pennsylvania.

Baurmeister, Carl Leopold von, ed. Bernhard Uhlendorf (1957). *Revolution in America: Confidential Letters and Journals 1776–1784 of Adjutant General Major Baurmeister of the Hessian Forces.* New Brunswick, NJ: Rutgers University Press.

Burgoyne J. (1780). *State of the Expedition from Canada, As Laid Before the House of Commons.* London: J. Almon.

Cannon, Richard (1851). *Historical Record of the Forty-Sixth or the South Devonshire Regiment of Foot.* London: Parker, Furnivall & Parker.

Cecere, Michael (2007). *They Behaved Like Soldiers: Captain John Chilton and the Third Virginia Regiment.* Westminster, MD: Heritage Books.

Court Martial (1864). *Proceeding of a General Court-Martial, Held at Brunswick, in the State of New-Jersey, by Order of His Excellency Gen. Washington [...] for the Trial of Major-General Lee.* New York, NY: J.M. Bradstreet & Sons.

Dann, John C. (1980). *The Revolution Remembered: Eyewitness Accounts of the War for Independence.* Chicago, IL: University of Chicago Press.

Daves, Edward Graham. (1893) *Maryland and North Carolina in the Campaign of 1780-1781,* Baltimore, MD: Peabody.

Dawson, Henry B., ed. (1867). *The Historical Magazine.* Morrisania, NY.

Denny, Ebenezer (1859). *Military Journal.* Philadelphia, PA: J.B. Lippincott & Co.

Drewe, Edward (1786). *Military Sketches.* Exeter: B. Thorn & Son.

Elmer, Ebenezer (1911). "Extracts from the Journal of Surgeon Ebenezer Elmer of the New Jersey Continental Line, September 11–19, 1777," in *Pennsylvania Magazine of History and Biography*, Vol. 35 No. 1. Philadelphia, PA: Historical Society of Pennsylvania.

Ewald, J. von, trans. & ed. J.P. Tustin (1979). *Diary of the American War: A Hessian Journal.* New Haven, CT: Yale University Press.

Fitzpatrick, John C., ed. (1934). *The Writings of Washington from the Original Manuscript Sources, 1745–1799. Vol. 12.* Washington, DC: Government Printing Office.

Greenman, Jeremiah, ed. R.C. Bray & P.E. Bushnell (1978). *Diary of a Common Soldier in the American Revolution: An Annotated Edition of the Military Journal of Jeremiah Greenman.* DeKalb, IL: Northern Press.

Groves, Lt-Col Percy (1903). *Historical Records of the 7th or Royal Regiment of Fusiliers.* Guernsey: Frederick B. Guerin.

Gruber, Ira D. (1997). *John Peebles' American War: The Diary of a Scottish Grenadier, 1776–1782.* Stroud: Sutton.

Hammond, Otis G., ed. (1930). *Letters and Papers of Major-General John Sullivan, Volume I, 1771–1777.* Concord, NH: New Hampshire Historical Society.

Higginbotham, Don (1985). *George Washington and the American Military Tradition.* Athens, GA: University of Georgia Press.

Howe, Sir William, ed. B.F. Stevens (1890). *General Sir William Howe's Orderly Book at Charlestown, Boston and Halifax, June 17, 1775 to 26 May 1776.* London: B.F. Stevens.

Hunt, Gaillard (1892). *Fragments of Revolutionary History.* Brooklyn, NY: Historical Printing Club.

Hunter, A. & E. Bell, eds (1894). *The Journal of Gen. Sir Martin Hunter, G.C.M.G., G.C.H. and Some Letters of His Wife, Lady Hunter.* Edinburgh: Edinburgh Press.

Laurens, John (1867). *The Army Correspondence of Colonel John Laurens , in the Years 1777–8 .* Albany, NY: The Bradford Club.

Lee Papers (1873). *Collections of the New York Historical Society for the Year 1872, Vol. 2.* New York, NY: New-York Historical Society.

Lee, Henry (1824). *The Campaign of 1781 in the Carolinas: With Remarks Historical and Critical on Johnson's Life of Greene ...* Philadelphia, PA: E. Littell.

Lee, Henry (1869). *Memoirs of the War in the Southern Department of the United States*. New York, NY: University Publishing.

McCullough, David (2001). *John Adams*. New York, NY: Simon & Schuster.

Mackenzie, Roderick (1789). *An Address to the Army in Reply to Strictures on Tarleton's History of the Campaigns of 1780 and 1781*. London: James Ridgeway.

McMichael, James (1892). "Diary of Lieutenant James McMichael, of the Pennsylvania Line, 1776–1778," in *Pennsylvania Magazine of History and Biography*, Vol. 16 No. 2. Philadelphia, PA: Historical Society of Pennsylvania.

Marshall, John (1925). *The Life of George Washington, Volume 2*. New York, NY: William Wise.

Martin, James Kirby, ed. (1993). *Ordinary Courage: The Revolutionary War Adventures of Joseph Plumb Martin*. New York, NY: Brandywine Press.

Martin, Joseph Plumb. (1962) *Private Yankee Doodle*. Boston, MA: Little, Brown & Co.

Moore, Frank (1860). *Diary of the American Revolution, Vol. I*. New York, NY: Scribner's.

Myers, Theodorus Bailey (1881). *Cowpen Papers*. Charleston, SC: News & Courier.

Peterson, Harold L. (1956). *Arms and Armor in Colonial America, 1526–1783*. Harrisburg, PA: Stackpole.

Pickering, Octavius (1867). *The Life of Timothy Pickering*. Boston, MA: Little, Brown & Co.

Reed, Joseph, ed. W.B. Reed (1847). *Life and Correspondence of Joseph Reed*. Philadelphia, PA: Lindsay & Blakiston.

Scull, Gideon Delaplaine, ed. (1881). *The Montresor Journals*. New York, NY: New-York Historical Society.

Seymour, William (1883). "A Journal of the Southern Expedition, 1780–1783," in *Pennsylvania Magazine of History and Biography*, Vol. 7 No. 3. Philadelphia, PA: Historical Society of Pennsylvania.

Seymour, William (1995). *The Price of Folly*. London: Brassey's.

Shaw, John R. (1807). *A Narrative of the Life and Travel of John Robert Shaw, the Well Digger*. Lexington, KY: Daniel Bradford.

Simcoe, Lieutenant Colonel J.G. (1844). *Simcoe's Military Journal*. New York, NY: Bartlett & Welford.

Smith, Samuel Stelle (1976). *The Battle of Brandywine*. Monmouth Beach, NJ: Freneau Press.

Stewart, Major-General David (1825). *Manners and Present State of the Highlanders of Scotland*. Edinburgh: Constable & Co.

Stone, W.L., ed. (1882). *Orderly Book of Sir John Johnson during the Oriskany Campaign, 1776–1777*. Albany, NY: Munsell's Sons.

Syrett, Harold G. and Jacob E. Cooke, eds (1961). *The Papers of Alexander Hamilton, Vol. 1*. New York, NY: Columbia University Press.

Tarleton, Lieutenant-Colonel Banastre (1787). *A History of the Campaigns of 1780 and 1781, in the Southern Provinces of North America*. Dublin: Colles, Exshaw, et al.

Ward, Christopher L. (1941). *The Delaware Continentals*. Cranbury, NJ: Scholar's Bookshelf.

Watson, Winslow C. (1856). *Men and Times of the Revolution: or Memoirs of Elkannah Watson*. New York, NY: Dana & Co.

Weedon, General George (1902). *Valley Forge Orderly Book of General George Weedon*. New York, NY: Dodd, Mead.

Wells, Henry (1834). Pension Application. Washington County, Pennsylvania.

Wilkin, Captain W.H. (1914). *Some British Soldiers in America*. London: Hugh Rees Ltd.

Williams, Catherine Read (1839). *Biography of Revolutionary Heroes: Brigadier General William Barton and also of Captain Stephen Olney*. Providence, RI: Putnam & Sons.

Williams, Richard (1954). *Discords and Civil Wars: Being a Portion of the Journal by Lieutenant Williams of His Majesty's Twenty-Third Regiment While Stationed in British North America during the Time of the Revolution*. Buffalo, NY: Easy Hill Press.

Young, Major Thomas (1843). "Memoir of Major Thomas Young," in *The Orion: A Monthly Magazine of Literature and Art*. Athens, GA: William Richards.

INDEX

References to illustrations are in bold.